PATIENT POWER! THE SMART PATIENT'S GUIDE TO HEALTH CARE

Smart patients don't just know about health and illness – they've got a handle on the health care system and know how to make it work for them. In *Patient Power!*, two health professionals give you the low-down on who is involved, what they should and should not do, and what happens.

Patricia and Arthur Parsons break down the health care system into three areas: the people, the process, and the results. 'The People' introduces you to a whole cast of characters: doctors, nurses, technical people, allied health professionals, and some of the people who offer alternative approaches to health care, explaining what each of these professionals does and the language they use. 'The Process' demystifies common diagnostic tests, how drugs are prescribed, high tech medical equipment, and what happens in the operating room after you go to sleep. 'The Results' gives you an insider's view on issues such as medical ethics, overuse of the system, social problems that have been made into medical problems, and having a 'smart' death.

Entertaining, informative, and easy to read, *Patient Power!* will give you the power to control what happens to you in the health care system.

PATRICIA PARSONS is a medical communications specialist and an Associate Professor in the Department of Public Relations, Mount Saint Vincent University, Halifax, Nova Scotia.
ARTHUR PARSONS is a family physician in Halifax. The Parsons are co-authors of three previous books including *Hippocrates Now! Is Your Doctor Ethical?*

PATRICIA PARSONS, BN, MSc
ARTHUR PARSONS, MD

Patient Power!
The Smart Patient's Guide
to Health Care

UNIVERSITY OF TORONTO PRESS
Toronto   Buffalo   London

© University of Toronto Press Incorporated 1997
Toronto Buffalo London
Printed in Canada

ISBN 0-8020-7186-4 (paper)

Printed on acid-free paper

Canadian Cataloguing in Publication Data

Parsons, Patricia Houlihan
    Patient power : the smart patient's guide to health care

ISBN 0-8020-7186-4

1. Medical personnel and patient. 2. Medical care.
3. Consumer education. 4. Patient education.
I. Parsons, Arthur H. (Arthur Hedley), 1943– .
II. Title.

R727.3.P36 1997   610.69'6   C96-931858-8

University of Toronto Press acknowledges the financial assistance
to its publishing program of the Canada Council and the Ontario
Arts Council.

We humbly dedicate this book to all the patients who have been our greatest teachers, and to our son, Ian Patrick Parsons, who inspires us to keep our dream alive.

Contents

List of Tables

Once upon a time ...

... there was a doctor and a patient. Perhaps the patient was you; perhaps the doctor was one you know. This was a smart doctor who knew that the best patient was a well-educated one. This patient was smart, too. He knew that being well educated about health care in general, and his own health care in particular, helped him to take his responsibility for his own health care seriously. This made the patient happy because he knew that being smart when it came to his health care empowered him; it put him in control. Believe it or not, in this situation, the doctor was happy, too. The doctor knew that he had a knowledgeable partner in decisions that would affect this patient: this partner was the patient himself. He would not be left to shoulder the burden of decision making for a patient who could and should be in charge of his own health. What a relief for the doctor!

In the sixteenth century, Francis Bacon said, 'Knowledge is power.' Some four hundred years later in a 1962 address at Berkeley, John Fitzgerald Kennedy said, 'In a time of turbulence and change, it is more true than ever that knowledge is power.' No time or place is more full of turbulence and change than health and medical care in North America in these, the last years of the twentieth century. It seems clear to us that people who are knowledgeable not only about their own health and illness, but also about how the health care system works, are the people who have power over their own lives as patients.

For years, in the doctor–patient relationship, it has been the doctor who has held the balance of power, primarily because he or she has been so much more knowledgeable about health and health care delivery than the patient. In this book, we invite you to learn some inside information about how the system works, and who makes it work and why, so that you may become an educated and thus empowered patient.

Doctors, nurses, and other health professionals live in a different world from everyone else. This world can be happy (new mothers with their new babies), heart-wrenching (the young child dying of cancer), appallingly stressful (the fifteenth disaster victim coming through the emergency room doors), risky (close contact with contagious diseases), exhausting (the young intern's thirtieth straight hour in the hospital), and frightening (the family doctor who is attacked in her private office). These people know a lot about some of the most intimate and intricate workings of the human body, sometimes yours. They study for years and have specialized jobs. They use odd-looking implements. Often they wear funny-looking clothing. These are also human beings, however, who laugh, cry, and sneeze, the same as everybody else does. They often talk in a language many outsiders – the patients – fail to understand. And so these outsiders stay there – firmly planted on the outside looking in, often at themselves, as they make their way through the maze that is the health care system of the 1990s.

If your knowledge of how the health care system works is confined to your visits to your own family doctor, perhaps a brief hospital stay, a visit to a sick friend or relative in hospital, and prime time television, then what you know is probably full of holes. We will help you fill some of those holes. We'll divide our discussion into three parts: the people, the process, and the outcomes.

Part 1, **The People**, introduces you to who does what and why. This section comes before the others, because the health care delivery system cannot function without those who give the care and make it work. A system of any kind is only as good as its people. These six chapters are like a playbill that familiarizes you with all the players: doctors, nurses, technical people, allied health professionals, and some of those who provide alternative treatment approaches. Because there are hundreds of different occupational groups providing specialized health care these days, it is important to develop a sense of who's who.

Part 2, **The Process**, looks at what these people can and should do for you, the health care consumer. First there is a translation of that foreign language that doctors, nurses, and other health professionals are privy to and that the average patient has difficulty understanding. Then the most widely used diagnostic tests are described, followed by discussion of what drug prescribing is all about, all that high tech medical equipment you might encounter, what happens in the operating room after you are asleep (and how you might avoid the knife, if possible), why a preventive approach may result in less need for illness care and, finally, how and why you might get a second opinion.

Part 3, **The Results**, helps you, the health care consumer, see the problems of the health care system as doctors see them. More than that, it helps you to deal with issues such as ethical dilemmas, overuse of the system and what that means to you, social problems that have been made into medical problems, and, when the time comes, how to have a 'smart death'.

Come with us and we'll take you by the hand behind the scenes to let you in on the real world of health and medical care. Although this world is a serious business, looking at it and learning about it needn't always be deadly. We'll introduce you to a cast of characters who represent the best and worst in health care today. These are people like you, your family, your neighbours, your colleagues, your doctors, and other health professionals you know or will come to know as you age. Together, you and these characters, with us as your guides, will become better educated about health care and be empowered as patients to get the best for yourselves.

PATTY AND ART PARSONS

AUTHORS' NOTE

This book is written as a docudrama. The characters and situations portrayed, although representative of reality as experienced by the authors, are purely fictitious. Any resemblance to real people or situations is entirely coincidental.

PART 1
THE PEOPLE

We often talk about the health care system as if it were a living, breathing entity, as if it has a personality of its own. The system is nothing without the people. It reflects the personalities, the knowledge, the skills, and the morals of those people. As a result of the fact that people make the health care system work, understanding the roles of its many workers is key to getting the best of what the system has to offer you when you need it. Come along with us and meet some interesting characters who play various roles in the health care system.

1

The 'Good' Patient

For some patients, though conscious that their condition is perilous, recover their health simply through contentment with the goodness of the physician.

Hippocrates, The 'Father of Medicine'

Wait a minute! Don't close this book in haste, thinking it ridiculous that in the 1990s being content knowing you have a 'good' doctor could somehow help improve your health. Stop. Think about this:

Smart patients are well-educated patients.
Well-educated patients have the power to get good health care.
Good health care is given by good doctors.
Therefore, smart patients have good doctors.

Your problem is to figure out how to be a smart patient. We are going to help you do that. But it may take a bit of time to educate yourself enough about your health care for you to have the motivation to take the steps necessary to find those good doctors (and nurses and physiotherapists and clinics and ...). Are you with us again?

'WHAT DO YOU MEAN you told him to get the hell out of your room, Dad? Dr Backman is the best bone surgeon in the city and you need him.' Eleanor Gass leaned over the side rail of her father's hospital bed and shook her head. 'Dad, when are you going to learn to be a good patient?'

Norman Oliver Thomas Frail brought all of his 75 years as straight up on the bed as he could, given that he had recently had his right hip replaced. 'Eleanor,' he began, 'you may have been my daughter for the past 45 years, and you may be pretty smart, but you don't know a damn thing about what it's like to lie in this bed and watch yourself wither away. When some young baby-faced doctor comes in with his gaggle of medical students and starts talking about me like I'm not even here, I get mad. And I've a right to be mad. Then they start poking me and using big words so that I can't understand what they're saying. A "good" patient? No, I won't be "good."' Mr Frail fell back on his pillows, exhausted.

Eleanor was astonished at the tone of her usually compliant father. 'You took a fit, didn't you, Dad?'

'I did what I had to do, if that's what you mean. I got their attention, I did. Then I fired Dr Backman.' Mr Frail was almost giggling.

'Dad, Dad,' Eleanor began again, shaking her head, 'if you could just be a good patient, we could get you out of here and home. Why can't you sit back and let the doctors and nurses do their jobs?'

Mr Frail shook his head. 'Let me tell you about good patients. I was a good patient once. When I had the heart attack ten years ago, I was a good patient. I listened to everyone, did what I was told, and never made a fuss. I was so mad all the time, every day I thought I'd have another heart attack. No, I'll tell you what a good patient is. A good patient is one who stays in charge, and I'm surprised you don't know that. I only wish I knew more about all this darned medical stuff. Then I'd really be a good patient. Give me that hospital directory. I'm going to find me a new doctor – one who'll listen to me. I might even let a woman doctor near me. What do you think of that?'

Eleanor didn't quite know what to make of anything her father had said this morning. She had never heard him talk like that before. She thought perhaps he was watching too much daytime television, with so much time on his hands. 'Imagine Dad taking charge like that! We're certain to be labelled problem patients at this hospital from now on,' she thought.

IS ELEANOR ALONE IN HER CONCERNS about patients being blackballed for being assertive? Not at all. What she doesn't understand, however, is that today's doctors respect a 'good' patient – if that good patient is good in 1990s terms, not 1950s terms.

Doctors in North American society used to be up on pedestals. They had the knowledge and therefore the power. They made decisions for us, because it was widely believed that they knew best. It wasn't just the doctors themselves who believed this; patients believed it, too. In truth, they really did know a great deal more than their patients. Times, as they say, have changed. Dramatically.

With the greater interest and emphasis on health and medicine, medical information is much more widely and easily available now. Although not all sources, such as the media, are to be relied on as absolutely accurate, they do provide a lot of material to make us question past approaches of accepting, at face value, what your physician does and says. Just because you question your doctor, however, doesn't make you a smart patient.

Patient power takes two things:

1 Knowledge about how health and medical care are delivered
and
2 The right attitude to make use of that knowledge to do yourself the most good.

Make yourself as informed as possible about any health problems you may have, and then leave the details of your illnesses to those who know the most about them, like your doctors, nurses, and other health care workers. You start by working on your understanding of how things get done in health care. For example, if you don't even know who these people are, what they do, and what part they play in your health care, it doesn't really matter how much you know about your diabetes, arthritis, heart disease, or anything else – it will never be possible for you to use that knowledge.

The second component of patient power is *attitude*. Your frame of mind will enable you to bridge the gap between simply possessing knowledge and putting that knowledge to work for you. The right attitude is the catalyst that begins the process of empowering you. Learn to develop that powerful attitude. It is a matter of making choices – choosing to play the passive patient or choosing to assertively (but not aggressively) use your patient power.

Let's first look at who the 'good' patient is, both from the doctor's point of view and from yours.

The historical 'good' patient

The history of a subject can often help us to understand why things are the way they are. It's possible to go back to Greece in the fifth century BC, to the time of Hippocrates, the Father of Medicine, to examine what patients and their attitudes were like then. For a more useful history of the 'good' patient, though, we need look no further than the beginning of this century.

At the turn of the century, the practice of medicine was just beginning to take on some of the characteristics that make it what it is today. One of those was the development of a solid system to educate doctors. Medical education in North America was coming into its own, and physicians had already attained a certain level of status within their communities. Medical care itself, however, was still only at the stage of caring rather than curing. Medicine could treat the symptoms of diseases but, because the underlying causes of diseases were generally unknown, there was little that doctors could do to prevent the symptoms from recurring: there was little in the way of cure. For example, a doctor could treat an elderly woman's broken leg, but could not do anything about the underlying osteoporosis that may have contributed to it.

Doctors had a fairly well-acknowledged monopoly on information about health and illness, at least as much of it as was known at the time by anyone. This level of knowledge gave them a very powerful role in the doctor–patient relationship. The possession of both knowledge and power led to what has come to be called 'paternalism' in health care: this 'father-knows-best' attitude was prevalent among turn-of-the-century doctors – and persists even now in some situations.

Many of today's older adults grew up in an era when the doctor's opinion was not questioned. The roles were fairly clear and well understood. The good patient listened to the doctor and did what he or she was told. The patient was compliant, unquestioning, and respectful. The doctor was all-knowing, powerful, and fatherly.

While there are still some patients who feel comfortable with this relationship, most do not. More worrisome, though, are the older (but occasionally younger) doctors who continue to feel more satisfied with the 'good' patients of old.

The modern 'good' patient, as defined by the doctor

One of the easiest ways to understand how doctors develop their own views of the 'good' patient is to begin by defining the 'bad' patient, the patient with whom the doctor would rather not have to interact.

If you walk into a room full of doctors and ask them to describe their most difficult, frustrating, worst patients, you would be startled to discover how often the same labels come up. The 'bad' patient is:

- a chronic complainer
- hypochondriacal
- non-compliant
- neurotic
- wimpy
- whiny
- demanding

Does this mean that doctors expect patients to be passive, acquiescent, uninvolved, stoic, and uncommunicative? Does the traditional doctor–patient relationship, characterized by a good deal of patient passivity and doctor activity still hold? Not really. The modern doctor isn't very comfortable with this relationship, either. Today's doctor, however, may not view a 'good' patient in the same way as you, the patient, does, either.

As we will discuss in chapter 2, doctors are educated to treat illness. In fact, they are not really 'health professionals' at all, but rather 'disease professionals.' Nurses have known this for years. As a result, to a doctor a good patient may be someone with an identifiable problem that preferably is physical (unless the doctor is a psychiatrist), amenable to treatment, and that can be cured using the arsenal of modern medical techniques that is available. This doctor can 'cure' you by using his or her specialized skills. This is very satisfying for the doctor. The problem is that, increasingly, many people who present themselves in a physician's office do not have such simply diagnosed and treated illnesses. Alarming numbers of them have physical concerns that are of psychological, and not physical, origin.

Consider this. Have you ever gone to the doctor with a cold? Your answer may be 'yes' and another person's answer may be 'no,' even though you both apparently had the same problem. Why will one person visit a doctor for a problem that another person leaves to time to look after? What makes this difference in behaviour? If you choose to see your doctor for a minor ailment that has no other cure but time, likely it is some other overriding need that takes you there, even if all your doctor says to you is to go home, get some rest, take an analgesic (painkiller), and drink lots of fluids. Probably you could have figured out that treatment without benefit of the doctor's years of education and experience. This doesn't mean, however, that you are any less in need of your doctor's services. It's just that your doctor is unlikely to be able to do anything for you. This situation can be frustrating for a physician who has been trained, and who has developed a mindset to cure, especially if the patient wants and expects something to be 'done.' The problem that develops here for medical care is that the doctor may feel the need to do more for you: to prescribe antibiotics, for example, 'just to be sure.' This leads to the likelihood that you will continue to go to the doctor whenever you experience cold symptoms, and it further leads to the beginnings of overuse of the health care system (more discussion about this in chapter 15). Whether this makes you a 'good' patient from the doctor's perspective depends on the doctor.

The composite modern 'good' patient, from the physician's point of view would be someone who

- is always on time for appointments and doesn't miss them without providing sufficient notice;
- is compliant with the recommended medical regimen, but this compliance is tempered by taking some responsibility for personal health;
- isn't a chronic complainer or hypochondriacal;
- shows respect and thoughtfulness (for example, doesn't call at all hours with minor problems);
- doesn't leave the most important reason for appearing in the doctor's office to the last few minutes, just as the doctor picks up the chart and begins to say 'good-bye' ('Oh, by the way, Doctor ... ').

At first glance, this doesn't seem to describe the empowered, smart patient that you might have in mind. Nevertheless, even though 'educated as a patient' is not on every physician's list of what makes a 'good' patient, when questioned, you are likely to find that a good doctor does, indeed, value the patient whose knowledge and involvement are above average.

The modern 'good' patient, as defined by the patient

We are going to take the point of view of the modern patient and suggest a more productive way to define the 'good' patient. The bottom line is that if you are a 'good' patient, as you might define it, you are a smart patient by definition. From the patient's point of view, then, what makes you a 'good' patient in today's health care system?

- You ask the right questions. This means that you keep yourself informed about your own health status.

- You take an active part in health care decisions that affect you. This follows from being informed. Now you use this information to ensure that your right to take part in the decisions affecting you is upheld.
- You know yourself well enough to understand your own value system. In other words, you know what's important to you when it comes to issues such as quality versus quantity of life.
- You don't rely on the health care system to be everything to everyone. You realize that there are some problems that the health care system can't fix, and you can't expect it to fix. Social problems, such as family disruption and financial problems, may result in health problems, but the root cause is still social, and the health care system can't cure them.
- You are assertive, determined, open-minded, flexible, and goal-directed.
- The bottom line is that you are empowered by knowledge and are not afraid to use it.

As an empowered patient you are a knowledgeable, assertive health care consumer who gets the most out of the system for the benefit of your health and your family's health. Your doctor, however, is really only representative of a much larger health care system that has many facets and, as we shall see in the next few chapters, many players. Get your score-card out, and get ready to take down their vital statistics!

2
Who's on First? Doctors?

There are only two sorts of doctors: those who practise with their brains, and those who practise with their tongues.

Sir William Osler (1849–1919)

The alarm clock on the small bedside table buzzed angrily by Dr Pete Kowalski's sleepy head. He awoke with a start, looked around groggily at the small intern's on-call room and recalled where he was. He threw himself back on the bed realizing that, once again, he probably wouldn't have time to shower this morning. Pete was to meet Dr Backman and the rest of the crew at the nursing station on 7 West promptly at 6:15 to make rounds. As usual, he would have to make a choice: eat or shower? Today, eating would get priority as he heard and felt the hunger pangs. He had missed dinner the night before because of a car accident after which the whole night had been one blur of activity.

Pete hadn't slept in thirty-six hours and, when he finally fell into bed at 3:30 a.m., his last thought was that he would have to get up again at 5:45. It was hardly conducive to sound sleep.

He arose quickly, threw some water in his face, changed his grubby 'greens' (that many of the interns and residents used as much for on-call pyjamas as for the operating room) for a set of clean ones, pulled on his lab coat, shoved his wallet in his back pocket, notebook and stethoscope in his lab coat pocket, ran a toothbrush over his teeth, and bounded out of the room toward the stairwell that led to the cafeteria.

'Hey, Pete,' he heard as he gulped his coffee and rubbery boiled egg. 'You look awful. You really should try to get more sleep!'

The cheery voice was that of Pete's senior resident, Dr John Campbell-Wallace III, who had only three more months left in his orthopaedic surgery residency before heading out to the real world of private offices and fat fees. John came from a long line of medical men and women. With his mother a psychiatrist and his father a heart surgeon, his grandfather a retired surgeon and his grandmother a society heiress, John seemed to have the world by the tail. He was joining his parents' multispecialty practice, after his wedding and a month-long honeymoon in Europe. Pete hated the sight of John's well-rested, smiling face this morning.

While downing the last of his coffee and sprinting to keep up with John as they headed off to rounds, Pete was pondering the decisions he had made in his life. Most interns had little time for philosophizing, but lately Pete seemed to be devoting more and more of his attention to just such mental pursuits.

As long as he could remember, he had never wanted anything else but to be a doctor. He hadn't been born with a silver spoon in his mouth, which is the way he thought of John, but his story was not one of extreme hardship, either. He thought of himself and his life as fairly average. He had a mom, a dad, a sister, and a dog. He had played hockey, taken music lessons, studied just hard enough in high school to get into a decent university, and made good enough grades to be accepted into his second-choice medical school. He had had a girlfriend off and on through his four years in medical school, and he liked to have a few drinks late on Thursday nights at the medical fraternity. Most of his girlfriends had been nurses and physiotherapists, mainly because he didn't seem to have the time to meet anyone else. All his friends were med students, and he had long since given up hockey. He still strummed the guitar from time to time to relieve stress. For the past four years Pete had spent the vast majority of his waking hours, and a good number of his sleeping hours, in either the hospital or the medical library. In taking stock, he realized that he had led a very sheltered life. Now he was wondering: Was it all worth it?

Last night he might have said no. This morning, however, after two hours of sleep, he was beginning to get giddy, and even Dr Backman was starting to look good.

WE'LL REJOIN PETE AND THE OTHERS on rounds shortly, but first let's look at doctors, among the premier members of your medical team.

So many different kinds ...

Like the offerings on a huge restaurant menu, there seem to be so many different kinds of doctors. Trying to figure out who they are, what they do, and how they might be of use to you as a health care consumer is work worth doing. It's a little like trying to identify features of a puzzle piece when there are 1000 pieces to put into place.

Let's look at doctors by dividing them into groups.

- Those who are still in their formal medical learning programs:
    Medical students
    Interns
    Residents (junior, senior)
- Those who have finished their formal medical learning programs:
    General physicians
    Specialists
    Subspecialists

Physicians are your most usual entry point into the health care system today. Whether by making an appointment or by ending up as an emergency admission to a hospital, you are much more likely to see a doctor than you are to see any other health care worker. You may then be referred to another professional, but usually a doctor starts off as your primary caregiver. (We'll explore this concept more when we talk about today's nurses.) Physicians as a group also see themselves as the one health profession responsible for the coordination of care, a role that has been challenged by other health professionals, notably nurses.

Doctors 'in training'

When you examine those diplomas on the wall in your doctor's office, have you ever considered what they really represent? If you have never looked closely at them, perhaps you should. The Latin may throw you a bit, but the diploma represents the completion of a lengthy formal education process. Let's look at what this diploma means.

First, the medical degree implies that the doctor who holds it has completed at least enough arts and science courses in college or university to gain entrance into medical school. Second, it means that the doctor has met the minimum requirements for graduation from medical school. The doctor's licence to practise is a separate document.

The premedical education is what prepares the doctor-to-be for what lies ahead in medical school. For many years, North American medical schools have placed great emphasis on the ability of an applicant in the area of science. This makes some sense as the medical curriculum has been very 'medical science' oriented. Thus, success in university science courses has been considered a fairly good predictor of success in medical school science courses. The second area of emphasis is on marks. Medical schools have traditionally looked for high achievers in both the premedical studies as well as on the standardized tests, the *Medical College Admission Tests* (MCAT), which have long been used by medical schools in both the United States and in Canada.

Times are, however, changing. Many medical schools of today are beginning to recognize the *art* of medicine. This art requires individuals who are, perhaps, better rounded. The highest achievers in the premedical sciences might not bring to the doctor–patient relationship the kinds of personal characteristics valued in modern medicine. Nevertheless, most physicians in practice today were educated in a system that emphasized science over the arts. This emphasis explains, at least in part, the way they make decisions in some circumstances.

Another sign of the times is the way medical schools and their curricula are changing. In years past, medical students were sub-

jected to hours upon hours of didactic lectures based on the somewhat artificial division of the body into systems. This meant that
a medical student would begin by studying the basic medical
sciences such as anatomy, including a good deal of dissection, to
see the structures of the body, physiology with labs to understand how the body works, microbiology with its labs to see how
micro-organisms, cells, and tissues grow and develop, and biochemistry and its labs to understand how the chemistry of the
body affects its functioning. Then, they went on to study the
body and its problems, system by system. So they studied the
circulatory system, the respiratory system, the gastrointestinal
system, the musculoskeletal system, the urinary system, and the
reproductive system. What this did in the minds of the fledgling
doctors was, essentially, to divide patients into their component
parts, from molecules and chemicals to organs and systems. This
left little opportunity to think in terms of the whole person. Some
North American medical schools have recognized this problem
and have begun experimenting with a more 'holistic' approach
to teaching medicine. This often involves a more case-oriented
focus, which might work something like this:

First-year medical students are divided into study groups led
by a tutor who is a practising physician. Throughout the year,
this tutor guides the students through a series of patient case
studies where many systems and problems are examined together.
The hypothetical patients might include someone with several
interacting physical problems, presenting a pharmacological chal-
lenge, and with a social issue that is affecting the person's well-
being (for example, a patient with heart disease and psoriasis,
who has developed a sensitivity to one of his medications, and
who has just lost his job). This provides a powerful opportunity
for new doctors to change their basic framework for thinking
about patients as whole persons rather than as systems with
problems.

After four years (fewer in some places where the students also
study through the summers), the medical student graduates and
embarks on postgraduate medical training. At least a year or two
of this hospital-based training is a requirement for licensure. If

the new doctor chooses to specialize or subspecialize, this part of the training can last for four or five years or more.

Specialist or not?

Not all new doctors choose to specialize. For one thing, the family physician is in great demand. This can be the one member of your health team who truly knows your whole health history and who can be the thread of continuity for you, the patient, and your family. Say you have been seeing the same physician for most of your adult life with few, if any, medical problems, and suddenly you are confronted by a problem. It is likely you will be referred to a specialist who may then need further help from other specialists. None of these people knows you as well as your family doctor, who can then act as the coordinator and conduit for information. If you do not have a trusted family doctor, this role goes unfilled, and you may be left wallowing in a sea of confusion.

The rapid advances in medical science during this century have resulted in an increasing need for specialists in specific areas of medicine. Categorized simply, there are doctors who specialize in surgery and doctors who specialize in internal medicine. (Obviously there are others such as psychiatrists who really don't fit into these broad categories but we'll talk about them later.) Early in the century this was an important differentiation, but today it is usually insufficient. There still are 'general surgeons,' and 'general internists,' but these specialties have become increasingly subspecialized, requiring even longer periods of training. Table 2.1 gives you some definitions of specific types of specialties in medicine, table 2.2 the specialties in surgery, and table 2.3 other specialists.

In addition to these two broad categories of specialists, there are those that fall outside. Psychiatrists, for example, are neither surgeons nor internists. They are medical school graduates, physicians, who have gone on to specialize in diseases of the mind. This is in contrast to *psychologists* who are people who hold doctoral degrees in psychology. A psychologist is not a medical doc-

Table 2.1
Sample Medical Specialists

anaesthesiologist	anaesthesia
cardiologist	heart
dermatologist	skin
endocrinologist	glands
gastroenterologist	digestive system
hematologist	blood
hepatologist	liver
nephrologist	kidneys
neurologist	nervous system
oncologist	cancer
physiatrist	physical medicine and rehabilitation

Table 2.2
Sample Surgical Specialists

cardiovascular surgeon	heart and blood vessels
neurosurgeon	brain and nervous system
ophthalmologist	eyes
orthopaedist	bones
otolaryngologist	ear, nose, and throat
thoracic surgeon	chest
urologist	urinary tract

Table 2.3
Other Specialists

obstetrician–gynaecologist	reproduction and women's health
pediatrician	children's health
psychiatrist	mental health
radiologist	X-ray treatment and diagnosis

tor, but an individual trained only in psychology. Both psychiatrists and psychologists deal with mental problems, but their approaches may be very different. Some of this difference is explained by the way each group is educated. In addition, as a medical doctor, the psychiatrist is permitted to prescribe medication and generally focuses on the biochemical basis of mental illness. Both types of professionals use psychotherapy, but the psychologist is limited to non-pharmacological therapies such as psychotherapy and hypnosis.

Over the years, doctors and others have facetiously defined the difference between the generalist and the specialist in medicine as the specialist being the one with the smaller practice and the bigger house. Unflattering though this may be, it is true that specialists are paid at a higher rate than family doctors, but there are also income differences from one specialty to another. In general terms, those doctors in the 'cutting' specialties – that is, specialities that involve surgery – are paid at a higher rate. This can lead to problems in the health care system itself (more about this in chapter 15).

Professional problems and today's doctors

Doctors are not without their own set of professional problems. They have toppled off their pedestals at an alarming rate over the past decade or two, and today they face new issues that can affect the way they do their jobs. This can be a problem for you, the patient.

First, doctors are facing more and more competition for patients. No longer is it enough for them just to be good doctors. They find they need to redirect some of their energies away from the actual practice of medicine to focus on ways to attract patients to their practices and, in the case of specialists, to induce family doctors to refer patients to them. Each individual doctor may have the very best interests of his or her patients at heart. Nevertheless, this concentration on the marketing of a specific caregiver may not really contribute to better patient care. On the other hand, this notion of competition is not always all bad. It can result in a physician's making his or her practice just a bit more patient-oriented in an effort to make you happy. Doctors taking this approach might offer office hours based on what the patients say they need, health information through the preparation and distribution of patient newsletters, and special health education events for patients. These kinds of features might influence your choice of doctor.

Second, doctors are more and more concerned about litigation. Lawsuits directed against doctors are big media events. A physician who fears being sued may tend toward overtreatment of patients to the detriment of the health care system as a whole and of other patients who are awaiting services.

Third, doctors today are facing an ever increasing number of ethically treacherous situations. These are largely the result of advances in technology and the thorny problems of how to use technology. Often the question arises: Just because we can do a thing, should we do it? This question, essentially, remains unanswered (more about this in chapter 14).

Both Canadian and American physicians are facing problems with the overall health care system. Canadian physicians, whose fees are dependent on the decisions of the individual provincial governments, have had to face as much as a 22 per cent decrease in income over the past few years. Thus, more and more physicians, especially highly trained, young specialists, are fleeing south of the border to where the grass looks greener. Coupled with the recent decrease in medical school enrolments, this is causing medical associations across the country to make dire predictions of physician shortages in the future.

The greener grass south of the border, however, may be looking more like straw close up. 'Managed care' in the United States means that the control of health care is increasingly in the hands of large companies. Naturally, part of the corporate culture of these companies is to turn a profit. Turning a profit is frequently viewed as being in direct opposition to the aims of good medical care. Doctors in the United States are beginning to complain of many of the same things, such as interference in the practice of medicine, that Canadian doctors have been complaining about in recent years.

Doctors are only people, too

The bottom line is, regardless of what kind of a doctor you are dealing with, how many years of education that person has, and where that education came from, the doctor is only human. The doctor is not God (no matter what he or she may believe!). Let's look at some myths about doctors.

Myth 1   There is a specific doctor personality.
In general, doctors represent many different types of personality traits. There are those who are aggressive leaders, or happy-go-lucky party animals, or perfectionists. They have individual value systems that are the products of their pasts – their childhood experiences, religion, culture, schooling, and interests. No one personality is shared by all doctors. Medical education in past years may have contributed to such a notion because of the focus on sciences, but doctors are, after all, only human.

Myth 2   Doctors are primarily motivated by money.
As difficult as it may be for you to believe, by and large, doctors are not motivated primarily by money. Money matters can, however, play a big role in their decisions about where and how to practice. This is becoming an increasing problem as we move toward reformed health care.

Myth 3   Doctors are primarily motivated by altruism.
It is no more true that doctors choose medicine to give of themselves completely than it is that they are all motivated by money. Thus, they are motivated by a complex of factors, just like most everyone in the world.

Myth 4   Doctors would rather not be questioned by patients.
It used to be uncommon for patients to question doctors. They had little basis for doing so. Today, however, with the plethora of medical issues that are related in the media every day, patients often feel that they have a good deal of accurate information. The modern, 'good' doctor welcomes patient questions and the patient's role in decision making, but often doctors are not happy that many patients receive much of their information (and misinformation) from the media. The media's main functions are to inform and entertain; it is not the purpose of the media to educate in detail. Frequently media stories give patients a false sense of being educated, and doctors resent not the patient's questions, but the position the media puts them

in. This situation pits physicians against the media, and it can be difficult for your doctor to explain the difference between what the media has portrayed and the reality as it is known by medical professionals. Most doctors today do welcome a well-informed patient's questions.

Myth 5   Most doctors think they are God and like you to believe it, too.

With some notable, high-profile exceptions, most doctors today neither think they are God nor wish to be. The awesome responsibility of playing God is truly not what most of them bargained for in medical school. Those who do think that they are God need to be reminded that indeed they are not.

Your role in developing a 'smart' doctor–patient relationship

You can be a smart patient by taking some control of your relationship with your doctor. Don't let your own attitude about doctors get in the way of playing your part in developing a good relationship. Believe it or not, a simple thing like a thank-you note from a patient means a great deal to most physicians. It can favourably affect the doctor's opinion of you and could thus benefit you in many ways in the future. With all the negatives facing the medical care system today, a thank you may be the only good thing that happens to a doctor in the course of a day.

You can improve your relationship with your doctor by asking, sincerely, 'How are *you* today, doctor?' Even though it might seem more appropriate for your doctor to be asking you this (and he or she will, we guarantee it), your doctor is a person, too, and it can be very draining to be giving of oneself all day long without any fuel. This simple question gives just enough back to your doctor's engine that you are likely to get a bit more out.

Occasionally, however, you may have reason to criticize rather than praise your doctor. Although you may want your doctor to be aware of your concern, you may not want to ruin the other parts of the relationship. You can criticize your doctor without ruining your relationship, but you need to do it skilfully.

First, ensure that you have complete privacy when you are criticizing your doctor. You should not be within earshot of any other patients or any other staff members. This is simple respect.

Second, the 'sandwich approach' often works nicely. This means sandwiching the criticism between good news. Clearly, if you are not sufficiently annoyed by the doctor's behaviour that you want to discontinue seeing him or her, then there are likely still many reasons why you believe him or her to be a good doctor. Use these reasons as your slices of bread.

Third, make sure you reproach the behaviour, not the person. If, for example, your criticism relates to the fact that you always have to wait an hour to see your doctor, direct your comments to this obvious scheduling problem, not to the doctor personally.

Finally, when asking for a problem to be corrected, don't demand. This can lead to considerable defensiveness, and you may have ruined your relationship.

As a patient, it seems that you never have the opportunity to evaluate your physicians. No one gives you a score-card to grade them on. Every once in a while, however, someone does, indeed, take the time to ask patients what they think. In the early 1980s, the late Dr Norman Cousins conducted an informal survey of 563 people in the neighbourhood of the University of California at Los Angeles Medical School so that he could obtain some insights into what people like and don't like about their doctors. His findings probably echo, at least to some extent, thoughts you may have had about your doctor.

Dr Cousins found that 85 per cent of the respondents had either changed doctors or thought about changing doctors in the previous five years (this didn't include those whose physicians had moved, died, or retired). The reason for this, cited again and again, related not to the physician's medical abilities, but to the physician's ability to communicate (Cousins 1985).

Your doctor is usually your entry into the health care system. Good communication takes two. You may not be able to do anything about your doctor's communication skills, but there is little doubt that improving your own ability to communicate will improve at least half of that relationship.

Your doctor is a person. You need to see this. It can help you to take seriously your role in maintaining a positive doctor–patient relationship. The smart patient recognizes that each person in the relationship has a responsibility to maintain its integrity and that abdicating this responsibility gives back to the doctor the power that has traditionally been the hallmark of the unequal doctor–patient relationship.

3

Angels of Mercy? The Nurses

To be a good nurse one must be a good woman ... What makes a good woman is the better or higher or holier nature: quietness ... gentleness ... patience ... endurance ... forbearance.

Florence Nightingale (1881)

By the time they reached the seventh floor, Pete and his senior resident were joined by a junior resident in her first year of postgraduate studies in bone surgery, and two medical students who were just starting a rotation with Dr Backman. As they rounded the corner and came in sight of the nursing station, Pete noticed that Dr Backman was not yet in his normal position in front of the main computer screen, so he took a sharp left and detoured into a patient's room.

He knocked gently on the door. 'Mr Frail?'

'Pete! Come on in, boy. I've some things to tell you.'

Pete pushed the door open and went over to the bedside. He lowered the side rail and sat on the bed. Mr. Frail took his hand for a moment.

'Pete, I fired that Dr Backman. He's one pompous, egotistical fool of a man and I don't care how good a doctor he is. I don't want him around me.'

Pete started to interject in defence of his teacher, but realized that Mr Frail was closer to the truth than he liked to believe. Pete was well aware that Dr Backman was a terrific orthopaedic surgeon, but Pete himself had also spent the past month putting up with the great doctor's ego.

'By the way, Pete. I spied a new patient next door. Her name's Susanne something, and she looks like just your type. I'll put in a good word for you, if I happen upon her today. You really shouldn't spend so much time on your work.'

Pete smiled. In almost the final week of this month-long rotation through orthopaedic surgery, he knew that he would miss some of the patients, especially Mr Frail. Mr Frail was admitted in Pete's first week on the service and was the only patient still here. They had become quite close in those weeks, and Mr Frail always asked him how he spent his time off. Pete didn't mind talking to him about it; he knew that Mr Frail was thinking of his own youth.

'I'll have to meet this Susanne,' Pete said with a smile, as he rose from the bed, put up the side rail, and opened the door. 'Got to get to rounds with you-know-who. We'll talk about Dr Backman later.' And he was gone.

Next door, Susanne MacDonald was trying to reach her call bell that had fallen on the floor. Now that her surgery to set her badly fractured femur (upper leg bone) was two days behind her, she was feeling much better, but frustrated that she couldn't move around more.

Just then a young woman dressed in a pale blue uniform came through the door holding a specimen bottle.

'We'll need a urine specimen this morning, Susanne.'

Although the young woman knew her name, Susanne had never seen her before. She didn't introduce herself. Susanne supposed she was a nurse. She had been here for two days and didn't know one nurse by name. She didn't even know which of them were nurses at all.

Susanne had fallen from a horse and massively fractured her leg. It had required some pins to be inserted during an operation to stabilize it. This had been expertly performed by Dr Backman and company. Shortly after she had been admitted directly from the operating room, a 'nurse' in a white pant suit had come in and taken her blood pressure, temperature, and pulse, marked the numbers on a sheet of paper, and, without a word, left the room.

Shortly after that, yet another 'nurse' dressed in white with a deep pink apron had come in to pour her a glass of drinking water and to chat about the weather. When Susanne asked if she would be her nurse for the day, the woman had laughed and said that she was the 'ward aide' but that there would be many, many nurses caring for Susanne during the next few days. The ward aide had not been wrong.

Susanne found it curious that very few of the hospital staff members ever introduced themselves by name, much less by occupation, and she discovered that the nurses could not be identified by sight either. They were no longer the white-clad angels of mercy with the ever-present black-banded cap. It was very confusing. Susanne herself was an ultrasound technician at another hospital in the city. She thought that she, more than most people, ought to know something about who's who on a hospital ward. At work, she didn't, however, spend much time on the nursing units. She had thought it must be awful for people who had no connection at all to health care; they must be puzzled constantly.

The next morning, Susanne had been awakened by an attractive young man who told her he would give her the pain medication Dr Backman had ordered. When she told him she didn't think doctors gave many needles in hospitals these days, he laughed and told her that he was the medication nurse on her 'team' that day. He was very good at giving needles, so Susanne thought he must be a good, if not conventional, nurse. A few minutes later, when she was beginning to feel a bit drowsy, a very young woman stopped at her bedside and introduced herself as 'Terri,' her student nurse. Terri told Susanne that she would be with her all day. A slightly older woman came in while Terri was talking to Susanne and introduced herself as Terri's nursing instructor. Although she wasn't the old battle-axe Susanne somehow expected to see as a nursing instructor, Susanne was very grateful just to know who these people were.

The first night after her operation was not as bad as Susanne had expected it would be. Her asthma, however, had begun to act up, and she had to be given medication by the night medication nurse, this time an older woman in white with a black-banded cap! So there were still some die-hards who wouldn't give up the cap.

The following morning, a young woman in a white lab coat over street clothes came in and told Susanne that she was a clinical nurse specialist who specialized in patients with lung conditions. Susanne thought she was a doctor, because she had never heard of this kind of a nurse. She assured Susanne that she was, indeed, a nurse, but had spent eight years in university learning to be a specialist. Her name tag called her 'Doctor,' but she assured Susanne that she held a PhD, not an MD. She was a doctor of nursing. Susanne had no idea what to expect of this nurse.

Just as Susanne was contemplating all of this confusion, Dr Backman and his crew knocked on her door and entered in a gaggle. Susanne knew that they were on 'rounds.' By now she also knew that the thirty-fivish nurse, who seemed to be more in charge than Dr Backman, was the head nurse. Susanne had not caught her name, but at least she knew her rank!

THE TIME IS LONG PAST when you could say, 'a nurse is a nurse is a nurse.' Fifty years ago, most nurses had similar training, which took place in hospitals, and they carried out the same functions in hospitals. They did everything. They were responsible for the care of the patients, and also for the care of the hospital. They made and served meals for patients, cleaned, sterilized instruments, and bowed down to the physicians. Today, as a result of the increasing complexity of technology and sophistication in the health care industry, the nursing profession is, to many both inside and outside the health care system, almost unrecognizable.

Susanne's hospital experience is very typical of many patients in moderate-to-large size hospitals where a dizzying array of different kinds of nursing staff provide specialized nursing care. The jobs that these women, and increasingly men, do and what educational backgrounds they have are just two of the many changes and thus two of the factors that lead to confusion among many people.

Nurses make up the single largest group of health professionals in North America. But the term *nurse* is often misunderstood. Today's nurses work not only in hospitals, but also in
extended care facilities (nursing homes), industry (as occupational
health nurses), clinics, physicians' offices, schools, the community (as public-health nurses) and, increasingly, in their own private practices as nurse practitioners.

Nurses in history

It's almost two generations ago, in 1960, that Peggy Nuttale, an
American nurse, wrote a book entitled *Nursing as a Career*. Its
purpose was to provide those young women considering nursing as a career with information to assist them in their choice. To
set the stage for what was to follow, Nuttale began by identifying for readers what she considered the most important characteristics in potential nurses: 'Without a doubt the first and most
important characteristic of a good nurse is that she should like
people.' This sounds more than sensible for a health professional!
Nuttale went on to list other favoured characteristics. Among
them she included: a sense of humour, reliability, being good
with your hands, and being 'fit,' whatever that might have meant
in the 1960s.

There are many stereotypes of nurses that have evolved largely
as a result of their portrayal in mass media. We've seen nurses
on television in roles that have ranged from handmaiden of the
doctors on the early shows, to iron maiden in later shows like
'M*A*S*H.' Newspaper accounts of nurses have not generally
been flattering, either, as we are regaled with stories of negli-
gence, or worse. None of these public stereotypes really does
justice to the nursing profession, nor do they help you find out
more about the nurses who care for you.

Nurses in North America today are expected by their profession to be bright, assertive, technically skilled, empathetic, politi-
cally aware, and, now, university educated. The unquestioning
obedience to doctors that was prevalent in years past has gone

the way of the 'cap,' which for a long time symbolized the sub-servience of nurses.

Nurses, the people

The vast majority of nurses in North America are women: 98 per cent in fact, but this is changing. Each year sees a small increase in the number of men choosing to attend nursing school, but nothing like the numbers of women who have chosen to be doc-tors. Just as the increase in the number of women in medicine has changed that profession, so too will men have an as yet un-determined impact on nursing.

There are other interesting changes in the face of nursing. More and more new student nurses have selected nursing as a second career. Many have completed university degrees in other fields, have worked in a variety of disciplines, have raised families, or any combination of these, before deciding on nursing. This has resulted in a very different group of student, and then graduate, nurses. They are older and wiser, more mature, and better edu-cated than their forebears. These older and wiser students have more life experience, ask more questions, and take very little at face value.

Educating nurses today

Before we can discuss how nurses are educated, we need to de-fine the term 'nurse.' *Nurse* is a legal term that can really only be used by people who are 'registered nurses.' The use of the term is governed by provincial and state licensing legislation. There are other groups who are part of the nursing staff and who carry out some nursing duties, but anyone who is not a 'registered nurse' is really not entitled to call her or himself a 'nurse.' We'll start by looking at how people get to be 'registered nurses.'

For many years, nurses have struggled to define their role and to determine what kind of education is ideal. Although you may have a general idea of the kinds of jobs nurses do in hospitals, you may be unaware of how nurses have come to see their role and therefore their educational requirements.

Nurses define what they do not only in terms of the traditional 'nursing care' that you would recognize in the hospital, but also in terms of preventing illness, providing health education, and supporting patients and their families in a wide variety of health-related situations.

They are involved in teaching patients and their families (such as the nurse who teaches the prenatal classes), providing counselling (such as the high school health nurse), and treating people as whole individuals rather than simply as a dressing to be changed or a medication to be given.

Increasingly, nurses see themselves as an ideal entry point into the health care system, although doctors currently play this role much more frequently.

Today nurses receive their education in a number of different ways. The nurse with a diploma is still the most common type of registered nurse in North America, but increasing numbers of nurses take their education in a four-year university program. Schools that prepare registered nurses at the diploma level vary widely in their philosophy and approach. Many, notably hospital-based programs, tend to value the more traditional views of discipline and structure, hallmarks of the past, while attempting to embrace the new theories, concepts, and technological advances. Others, especially those located in colleges, tend to take a more liberal view of education, allowing more self-directedness and reliance on the individual motivation of the student.

University nursing schools in both the United States and Canada provide a four-year program that leads to the Bachelor of Science in Nursing degree or, in some cases, Bachelor of Nursing (they are really the same thing). Nurses with these degrees are prepared for entry-level nursing positions, but they have spent more time during their educational programs in studying subjects with a broader base than nurses who have studied at the diploma level. In addition to taking the basic nursing courses, these students are also required to take a series of arts and science electives, more in-depth basic science, and advanced nursing courses that examine areas such as nursing administration, research, teaching, and community nursing. A nursing degree provides graduates with the opportunity to advance up the ladder of the nursing profession or to branch out into research or teaching after a period of experience as a staff nurse.

University preparation for nurses is the education of the future. In 1965, the American Nurses' Association determined that all professional nurses (registered nurses) must have an undergraduate (bachelor's) degree to be licensed. It is often difficult for the average person to understand why nursing leaders believe that the diploma programs are insufficient preparation for nurses today. Health care has, however, changed dramatically and nurses are playing roles outside the hospitals that seem to require a broader-based education.

Dr Judith Ritchie, a past president of the Canadian Nurses' Association, is very supportive of the need for further education of fledgling nurses. The holder of a doctorate in nursing, Dr Ritchie believes that, in addition to gaining further understanding of the health problems presented by patients in hospitals and other clinical settings, nurses need many other skills. She says emphatically, 'No other discipline would let someone run a department and control a two million dollar budget and thirty staff members with a diploma totally unrelated to the duties and the kind of critical thinking or other special skills needed.' Dr Ritchie is, of course, referring to those nurses who become head nurses and supervisors and are expected to have skills far beyond those of the average staff nurse, but who for years did not have any educational background to prepare them for the jobs. She thinks that nurses have done very well to have coped with the extra demands. But the time has come for change.

Registered nurses are the most visible and highly educated members of the nursing team. There are also several other categories of workers who provide a great deal of nursing care in hospitals, nursing homes, clinics, and other settings: practical nurses or nursing assistants. They are called different things in different places, including certified nursing assistant (CNA), registered nursing assistant (RNA) and licensed practical nurse (LPN). Regardless of title, their educational preparation is similar, although their responsibilities vary considerably with their work area.

The basic education for the CNA, RNA, or LPN is a ten- to twelve-month program offered in community colleges, hospitals, secondary or vocational schools, and special schools. The program focuses on the hands-on approach to basic nursing care, and these workers are frequently the ones who provide much of the care you receive as a patient. Under most circumstances though, the larger the hospital where they work, the less responsibility they are given. Nursing assistants who work in long-term care facilities, for example, tend to be given more responsibility than those in hospitals, primarily because there are fewer registered nurses employed in these settings. Usually, nursing assistants are answerable to the registered nurse for the care they give.

Despite the fact that in some situations nursing assistants can give similar care for less money, there has been some talk in the nursing profession of eliminating the use of nursing assistants. With the movement toward university education for all registered 'professional' nurses in North America, it seems that there may no longer be a place for these auxiliary health care workers. The most unfortunate issue for them is that there is no way they can advance up the ladder of the nursing profession without becoming registered nurses, and that means starting their education over again, usually from scratch.

You, the patient, will see these nursing caregivers giving bedbaths, changing bedpans, checking your intravenous tubing and solution, taking your temperature, pulse, and blood pressure, changing your dressing, completing your hospital chart, and sometimes even giving medications, although this varies with the work setting and location.

Nursing assistants, at present, provide a valuable service to patients in hospitals and other places where health care services are dispensed. You will see them frequently in physicians' offices and on nursing floors in hospitals and nursing homes. You will not see them in supervisory or teaching positions. Where you will see them in the future remains uncertain.

Where the jobs are

During her stay in hospital, Susanne began to realize that nurses perform a wide variety of functions and carry an assortment of titles. What follows is a list of the possible jobs you may find nurses of various types doing in hospitals or other places. Although this list covers many of the possibilities, there are new ones being added every year.

Staff Nurse

This is the most commonly held position in the hospital. This nurse is a registered or graduate (awaiting registration) nurse who has completed either a diploma or a degree program in nursing. This is the traditional role in which consumers see nurses providing care at the bedside. Many will move up through the ranks of nursing to higher positions, but the majority are staff nurses for the duration of their careers. There is currently a movement throughout North America for nurses who wish to practise their profession at this level to specialize and become expert caregivers in one particular area such as maternity nursing, nursing of heart patients, nursing of children, intensive care nursing, or any other specialty of medicine or nursing. A staff nurse is in charge of a nursing unit when the head nurse is off-duty.

Head Nurse

This is the first level of promotion for a staff nurse. Today this nurse usually has a four-year degree and experience as a staff nurse. The head nurse is responsible for directing the work of a group of nursing care workers ministering to a particular group of patients. To do this, the head nurse must organize work schedules, hire and evaluate staff members, oversee the unit budget, take some responsibility for the continuing professional development of the staff, and ensure that the patients receive quality care. These days it is unusual for a head nurse, or unit administrator as the position is sometimes called, to give direct patient care. In days past, the head nurse had more time for this bedside care. If you have a problem with any aspect of your care, whether it be with a particular staff member, or even with your medications, this is the first person you should seek. The head nurse of the unit is really in charge and

– keep this in mind – does not work for the doctors. The head nurse's boss is the Director of Nursing or, as is more common these days, the Vice-President for Nursing (and perhaps other things). The head nurse is an extremely good resource and an excellent go-between when you are trying to sort out problems with a doctor, but remember, she or he usually works only during the day from Monday to Friday. The nurse in charge of the unit at other times is generally one of the staff nurses on rotation.

Nursing Instructor

A nursing instructor in a diploma school of nursing has a minimum of a four-year university degree in nursing and perhaps a higher degree as well. An instructor of university nursing students normally has at least a master's degree (two years more university education beyond the bachelor's degree). In the clinical setting, this instructor is responsible for assigning, overseeing, and evaluating the care given by a group of student nurses. When not supervising students who are learning to give direct care, this individual is usually responsible for lecturing to the students in the classroom. University teachers may also be involved in research. If you have a problem with a student nurse (or if you want to commend a student), this is the person to speak with first.

Nursing Supervisor

A nursing supervisor was traditionally the nurse responsible for the entire hospital (or portion of a larger hospital) after hours, and that is frequently still the case. The supervisor is a nurse with considerable clinical experience who may or may not have a university education, but is at least a registered nurse. The nursing supervisor makes rounds to all the assigned nursing units during a shift and deals with staffing problems as well as individual patient or family problems if the staff nurses cannot handle them. On evening and night shifts, when the head nurse is not available, if you cannot have your problem solved by the staff nurse in charge, you should arrange to speak with the nursing supervisor.

Director of Nursing

Hospitals, nursing homes, and community health centres all have a nurse who is the boss. This person is frequently called the Director of Nursing, but may also be called the Assistant Executive Director or Vice-President, or by another title that reflects both how the facility is organized and the level of the position. As the titles imply, this is a very responsible position and is generally one of the highest in an institution, because nurses make up the majority of the workers in a health care institution. This person must be both an experienced nurse and an experienced administrator with an extensive educational background. Usually the director of nursing will hold a master's degree either in nursing or in hospital administration, and perhaps even a doctorate. This person has overall responsibility for the nursing department. Frequently, patients who are having difficulty with the nursing staff will complain directly to the director. This is generally not the most efficient way to make your feelings known, as someone closer to the situation can usually handle it. So try the head nurse or supervisor first.

Clinical Nurse Specialist

From a patient's point of view, this is a relatively new position in nursing. It is designed both to provide specialized expert care to patients and to provide staff nurses with a consultant in a specialized area that they may not deal with every day. A clinical nurse specialist usually holds a bachelor's degree in nursing as well as a master's degree in a clinical specialty and has considerable clinical experience in giving patient care. Clinical specialists are found most frequently in large teaching hospitals, but this role is filtering into smaller institutions, too. The majority of patients usually do not see this type of nurse. Some clinical nurse specialists in the United States choose to go into private practice. If you require nursing rather than medical care, you can opt to see a nurse and pay for her or his care on a fee-for-service basis which is usually considerably less than you would pay to be seen by a physician for the same thing.

Hospice Nurse
These nurses work with dying patients and their families. It is their responsibility to assist their patients to prepare for a dignified death. Terminal cancer patients constitute a large portion of their clients. Hospice nurses usually hold a four-year degree in nursing and have experience in dealing with death and dying. Also, they must possess the personal characteristics that make them effective caregivers for people in these situations. Some hospitals now have hospice units where dying patients can be cared for by these specialized nurses. Other hospitals provide this service on a consultation basis. If you believe that you or your family would benefit from hospice service, you should discuss the availability and appropriateness of a referral with either your doctor or with the head nurse. Some institutions also provide this care in the home.

Community Health Nurse
This person was traditionally called the public health nurse and provided care during home visits. In addition to that customary responsibility, community health nurses also visit schools and conduct immunization clinics. In many locales, it is also the responsibility of the community health nurse to teach prenatal classes for pregnant women. If you have a baby, you may be visited by your district's visiting nurse shortly after your release from hospital. A community health nurse today is required to have a university education in nursing, as this provides a broader knowledge base than a diploma. If you are in hospital and believe that you will need help on your discharge, there is usually a liaison nurse in the hospital who will see you and make the necessary arrangements. Ask your head nurse about this.

All of these are professional positions for registered nurses. In addition to nursing assistants, there are two other categories of nursing staff jobs that you may encounter.

Personal Care Workers
These individuals generally work in nursing homes or extended care facilities. They are trained at the institution by a short but

formal course and are qualified to give basic personal care. They assist the patient to care for hygiene (bedbaths, bedmaking), nutrition (feeding patients), elimination (bedpans, urinals, sometimes enemas), and grooming.

Nurses' Aides
These positions vary considerably from one institution to another. Trained on the job, nurses' aides do whatever unskilled work is required within the nursing department. Many nurses' aides are responsible only for functions such as cleaning bedsides and utility rooms and giving water to patients. Some are trained to assist the nurses with bedbaths and bedmaking. Bear in mind that these people usually have little or no formal training.

There are more nurses in the North American health care systems than any other single professional group. You might think that by virtue of sheer numbers, they would have the most power. Of course, you know that they do not. Doctors have traditionally had the upper hand. This, however, is changing, and nurses are becoming a force to be reckoned with.

There is clearly more to the nurses who are caring for you than meets the eye. If you are aware of their individual responsibilities, your stay in a hospital or other health care facility will be easier and less frightening. One of the most interesting roles that nurses can play for you is that of intermediary and interpreter. Consider the following scene:

You were admitted through the emergency department last night, suffering from what you considered to be severe chest pain. Four doctors and two nurses have just come into your room with your chart. You recognize the lead doctor as the cardiologist you saw briefly the evening before. He begins.

'Although it's really too early to say yet, we do not believe that there has been a myocardial infarct. You do, however, seem to have some ischemic changes to your heart muscle. We're going to run some more tests and then decide how best to treat this situation.'

Before you have a chance to open your mouth, he's gone, and one nurse remains behind to give you your medication.

'Did I have a heart attack?' you ask the nurse. 'Am I going to die?'

Then the nurse tells you that you didn't have a heart attack, but that the blood vessels to your heart muscle are showing some signs of narrowing. She tells you that, in its more severe stages, this is what does lead to a heart attack. She tells you that you will have another electrocardiogram and some more blood tests, and then you will be placed on some medication and a new diet to lower your blood cholesterol. You lie back relieved.

A nurse can be one of your best friends and collaborators, especially when you're in the hospital. Smart patients who understand the preparation and roles of today's nurses can use their expertise to understand more about what the rest of the health care team, particularly the doctors, plans and expects.

4

Hands Off! Those Technical People

The great tragedy of Science: the slaying of a beautiful hypothesis by an ugly fact.

Thomas Huxley (1825–95)

Mr Frail grumbled just loudly enough for the technician to hear. 'What was that, Mr Frail?'

'I said, I can't believe the number of people who stick things into you in hospitals.'

'You've been getting weekly blood specimens drawn for the past month, haven't you?' she asked as she expertly jabbed the needle into Mr Frail's arm. They both watched the vacuum in the test tube draw out the blood now slowly filling the clear tube.

'Just because someone always comes and jabs me doesn't mean I either understand or like it.' He looked at the tray of blood specimens she had placed on his over-bed table. There were several dozen tubes, with a variety of coloured tops. Some were red, some blue, some green. Mr Frail supposed that they meant something to the technician, but they meant nothing to him.

'What the heck happens to all that blood anyway?'

The technician snapped the tourniquet off his arm and smoothly removed the needle. 'Well, I take it to the lab, where some lab techs perform different tests on it.'

'Do those coloured tops mean anything?' he continued.

'Sure do. Some of those tubes have special chemicals in them to prepare the blood for specific tests.'

'There's an awful lot of tubes there! Don't you ever get one patient's blood mixed up with another? I've read about people being told they've got that AIDS virus when it was really someone else's blood that was tested.' He noticed that the technician was wearing rubber gloves.

She laughed. 'That isn't likely to happen, Mr Frail. We have a very well-developed identification method. We're very careful.' She was gently shaking one of the tubes she had filled with Mr Frail's blood. As she gathered up her materials, Mr Frail asked, 'Where'd you learn to take blood and identify it for the labs? Must take years to learn all that.'

'Actually,' she said proudly, 'I'm a biology student at the university. I took a week-long seminar on blood-taking and now I do this three mornings a week between 5 a.m. and 7 a.m. I'm planning to go to medical school.' She smiled.

As the technician left his room, Mr Frail wondered how a person could possibly learn all there is to know about blood-taking and keeping records and specimens straight in one week. One week! How much training did all those other technicians have? He didn't have time to consider this, though, as a stretcher was just making its way through his door with a hospital porter at the other end.

'Mr Frail?' asked the porter as he consulted a piece of paper in his hand. Mr Frail looked up.

'I'm taking you to Diagnostic Imaging.'

'What the hell is Diagnostic Imaging?' he asked with a scowl.

'I'm sure you've been there before in the past month. It's where X-rays are taken.' The porter busied himself helping Mr Frail get on the stretcher.

'Why the hell can't you say so, then? You know, it's pretty bad when even the porters speak a language no one understands. It's bad enough in the doctors.'

After a short trip through the hospital corridors and down three floors in an elevator, Mr Frail found himself waiting in a corridor. People buzzed around him. Just as he thought he might take a nap, as this was likely to be a long wait, a pleasant voice said, 'Hi. I think we're almost room-mates.'

Mr Frail looked up and saw Susanne from the room next to his. She was also confined to a stretcher, waiting and waiting.

They introduced themselves, and he sized her up for Pete. Then, of course, the conversation turned to hospitals, waiting, and all the different types of workers who sped by. Mr Frail soon found that he had a very knowledgeable companion, as Susanne was actually an ultrasound technician who worked at a hospital across town. Because she was able to see their identification and their uniforms, she began pointing people out to him.

'You must know everything about hospitals if you work in one.'

'Well,' Susanne began, 'I thought I knew a lot more than I do. You see, since I'm a technician, I work in a very specialized area. I know what most of these people in this department do because I work in one that's very similar. But, you know, I thought that I'd know more about the nursing staff than I do. I guess I'm at just as much of a disadvantage as any other patient when it comes to what happens on the nursing units. I just wish they'd introduce themselves.' She shook her head and then continued with Mr Frail's personal guided tour of the personnel in the Diagnostic Imaging Department.

'She's an X-ray technician. She uses that X-ray equipment to take X-rays. He's a student in the X-ray program. Oh, she's a radiology resident. You know, a doctor who's specializing in this X-ray stuff to diagnose and treat people. I've seen her at my own hospital for meetings recently. He's a blood bank technician. I wonder what he's doing over here?'

Mr Frail was just getting to asking Susanne about some details when they came to take him for his X-ray.

Technological advances in medicine

Truly amazing technological advances have been made in medical care and diagnosis in the past few decades. Never before have doctors had at their disposal such an array of machinery and approaches to find out what is wrong with you and with which to treat that condition. Without a doubt technology has improved medicine. It has, however, also caused some problems. We aren't going to discuss the pros and cons of technology. What we are interested in is how the technology that now exists in hospitals and other health care settings is affecting you when you are a patient, and how you might better understand it.

One of the most important single outcomes of all this advancement in medical technology for you as a patient is that with almost every new advance, every new piece of equipment, has come the development of yet another type of technical health professional. There have to be individuals who have specialized training to use this new technology. Your problem often becomes trying to determine just exactly who these people are and what you can reasonably expect of them so that you can be a smart patient.

When we look back at the history of technology in medicine, it is certainly clear that the twentieth century has seen almost all of it. The advances in diagnostic technology help your doctor to find out what's wrong with you. The advances in therapeutic technology are used to treat you. Now you need to know something about those people who use all of this new technology.

The people behind the technology

Medical technology is of no use to any of us if no one knows how to use the equipment and techniques involved. Thus, along with these developments, there has been a proliferation of technical workers. But just what *can* you expect of these technical people? How are they trained? Where do their jobs begin and end?

Technical people work in quite a few different places around a hospital or clinic. In general terms, they are just about everywhere, but there are more in some places than others. For example, most of the people who work in laboratories testing blood and other samples (such as urine, bone marrow, and bodily secretions) are technicians. They frequently work under the supervision of a medical doctor who has specialized in laboratory medicine. It's not quite that simple, though, because there are many different types of labs. The size and variety of the labs are related to the size of hospital and the type of service it provides. For example, tissue typing of a blood specimen might only be done in a large, regional hospital laboratory where they need this type of information for organ transplant matching and paternity testing. In addition, there are also private laboratories.

If you take a walk through the laboratory wing of a large, local hospital you will see a variety of different names on the doors leading to labs that contain different types of equipment.

The biochemistry lab examines the chemical make-up of specimens. A urinalysis, for example, is primarily a chemistry test (although the technicians doing a urinalysis also look for micro-organisms, and a special urine specimen must be taken and examined in microbiology to identify the organism present). It looks at the chemicals in the urine. The technicians report their findings, and the doctors make a judgment about how the results compare with normal and make a diagnosis. There can be a number of subspecialized chemistry labs.

Technicians in microbiology labs are responsible for finding micro-organisms (bacteria, viruses, fungi) in specimens. If you go to the doctor with a sore throat, for example, and he or she swabs your throat, the microbiology department is where that swab is sent for analysis. The technicians culture the specimen (place some of the secretions on a special medium) and look to see what grows. They then send a report of the observations back to a physician who interprets them for you. There are also subspecialty micro labs such as virology (the study of viruses) and various community health labs that specialize in culturing milk and water. Laboratory technologists also work in the blood bank determining blood groups, in the tissue-typing lab, in pathology, in histology, and various other places.

As a patient in a hospital, you will rarely see a lab technician. The person who takes your blood specimen might be an actual, trained technician, but more likely he or she is the type of individual that Mr Frail encountered (even though the particular hospital may call these people venipuncture technicians, they would have only the training described). Most technicians are truly hands-off health care workers. Their work relates to the specimens that they receive and are charged with testing. They occupy labs that may or may not be physically attached to the hospital, and they spend their days poring over microscopes and an array of other specialized equipment. Although lab technicians are critical to your diagnosis and treatment, and are considered part of the health team, nevertheless, they are very much silent members as far as you, the patient, are concerned.

The other major setting for technicians is what is now called the 'diagnostic imaging' department. Formerly the X-ray department, this area of the hospital was renamed to reflect the changes in what goes on there. Since Wilhelm Roentgen discovered X-rays in 1895, ways of looking at the inner areas of the body using his discovery and advances on it have developed incredibly with regard to both safety and usefulness. The types of tests that are performed now use not only X-ray technology, but also newer approaches such as MRI (magnetic resonance imaging), radioisotope scanning, and ultrasonography.

The technicians in these areas are subspecialized as well. They are responsible for using the equipment to either diagnose or treat you. Their patient contact is greater than that of the lab technician, though, as it is these technicians who will actually do the test. What really makes them hands-off people (using our definition) is the fact that they are not responsible in any way for your care, only for your test. You are unlikely to develop a long-term relationship with a technician in one of these departments. One possible exception to this is patients receiving radiation treatment for cancer, who return day after day to the same facility.

Technical staff in the diagnostic imaging department have responsibilities similar to those in labs. They are responsible for using the equipment to take the test and producing a hard copy with results. This copy is given to a physician who is responsible for interpreting the test results to make a diagnosis. This is important as we begin a discussion of what you could reasonably expect a technician to do or say. It is the doctor's, not the technician's, responsibility to draw a conclusion from the test. Technicians are not trained to make diagnoses, even though they may have picked up quite a bit of useful information over time.

While some technicians may be willing to discuss what they see, others are not and you can't reasonably expect them to do so.

There are also other places in the hospital where you will find technical staff. In general, the more technically oriented a place is, the more likely it is that there will be technicians, which, of course, seems obvious.

Other technicians who work in diagnosis include electrocardiograph technicians who use the ECG (also referred to as EKG) machines to test the electrical conduction system of your heart, and the electroencephalograph technician who tests the electrical conduction in your brain.

In the operating room we find perfusionists who run the heart–lung machines (some of these technicians are called cardiopulmonary technicians) and the equipment to flush out organs for transplant, as well as anaesthetic technicians who assist the anaesthetist.

It's almost impossible to list and discuss every single type of technician. In general, most technicians are trained in two- or three-year programs in hospital settings or community colleges. Sometimes they hold university degrees in science. They do not, however, receive training in diagnosis. They are responsible for the technical aspects of performing tests and for ensuring that accurate reports are presented to doctors. Table 4.1 is a listing of some of the technical people you might meet in your journey through the health care system.

Getting the most from your 'technical' encounters

While it might be tempting to expect the technical people who provide health services to give you answers about the tests (because they are the ones you have captive at the time), as you might have concluded from the previous discussion, this is not really appropriate. Furthermore, a reliable technician will not provide you with such information. It is not the technician's job; they are not trained to do so. After years of experience, many technicians may have more ability to determine just what is going on in an X-ray or other test than a fledgling medical resident;

Table 4.1
Some Technical Health Personnel

This kind of technical health care worker ...	does this kind of work
cytologist	is an MD who has specialized in the study of cells (e.g., changes in cells that lead to cancer)
cytotechnologist	works with the cytologist to identify cells under a microscope
dialysis technician	provides dialysis treatments to patients with kidney failure
EEG technician	operates a diagnostic machine to measure electrical impulses in the brain
EKG technician	operates a diagnostic machine to measure electrical impulses in the heart muscle
nematologist	is an MD who specializes in diagnosing and treating diseases caused by worms
nuclear medicine technologist	operates machines that use nuclear technology to diagnose and treat disease
perfusionist	operates perfusion machines such as heart–lung (may be called cardiopulmonary technician), dialysis, or organ-perfusion for transplant
phlebotomist	takes blood specimens (also known as a venipuncture technician)
pulmonary function technician	operates a machine to measure lung capacities
radiology technician	operates X-ray machines
ultrasound technologist	operates sonography (sound wave) machines

nevertheless, it is still not morally or legally right for technicians to give you this information. Your best approach here is not to even ask them to do so.

What, then, can you do to get the most out of your encounters with technical personnel? Just as discussed earlier with doctors, using the best people skills you can muster will go a long way in making your life in the diagnostic imaging department as smooth as possible. People there have the potential to make your life miserable. Here are some suggestions:

- Comply with any preparations that you are instructed about. If the instructions your doctor gives you indicate that you should not eat anything after midnight, follow them. Technicians cannot do their job properly with ill-prepared patients, and you could find yourself bumped to another time if you do not follow instructions.
- Tell the technician if you have any physical limitations that may cause you problems with the test or even the positioning of your body that is required. They don't usually have time to read your entire history, and if the doctor has neglected to mention this on the requisition for the test, it will go unnoticed.

Although they lack the high profile of the doctors and nurses on the front line of health care delivery, technical professionals are extraordinarily important to your health care – especially in these days of increasingly complicated technology. Technical personnel have a major role to play in the diagnosis, treatment, and interpretation of your health status. Smart patients know this and strive to understand the many specialized jobs these people do. Mr Frail may have had a hard time understanding their roles, but with a little bit of preparation you'll be ready for your next encounter.

5

Hands On! Some Others

'We've sent a consult to a podiatrist for you,' Terri told Mr Frail as she helped him to wash his feet. Terri's nursing instructor had now assigned her to care for both Susanne and Mr Frail.

Mr Frail looked puzzled. 'A what?'

'A podiatrist. He'll come to look at your feet and help you with those sore corns.' She looked at her watch. 'Oh, I almost forgot. I've got to get you to physio in fifteen minutes.'

Podiatrists, physios, and a whole lot of other names had become commonplace in Mr Frail's vocabulary over the past month. If he could just sort them all out. He made a mental note to talk to his daughter about this and find out whether he could continue some of this therapy at home when he was discharged. Mr Frail had decided that he was going to be discharged very soon. Although the doctors had yet to make this decision, Mr Frail had made it already. Dr Backman, whom he had reinstated as his doctor after much pleading on his daughter's part, had told Mr Frail that he could be discharged soon if arrangements could be made for his continuing care. He intended to move heaven and earth to make sure it happened.

Just then Pete strolled in through the door.

'Good morning, Dr Kowalski,' Terri said brightly. 'Mr Frail has to be in physio in fifteen minutes.'

'No problem,' Pete said, smiling. 'Mr Frail, I've made arrangements for the social worker to come to see you about home arrangements. Also, an occupational therapist will visit to do an assessment.'

'I'll miss you, Pete. By the way, you look worse today than you did yesterday. Have a bad night?'

'I didn't get much sleep for the third night in a row. I wasn't supposed to be on call again, but one of the other interns came down with the flu. It just didn't seem right for one of the doctors to vomit in the middle of surgery, so I had to assist Dr Backman with two emergency operations.'

Just as Terri returned to ready Mr Frail for his trip to the physiotherapy department, Dr Backman opened the door and entered, flanked by a resident and two medical students. He had a commanding presence. Mr Frail sighed and remembered that he had promised his daughter he would try to be agreeable.

'I see that Dr Kowalski has beat me to you this morning, Mr Frail,' he said peering not at Mr Frail but at his chart. 'It looks like we'll be able to send you home very soon as we discussed.' Still looking at the chart, he continued. 'Your therapeutic regimen requires further consideration on Dr Kowalski's part, but I'm certain we can make appropriate arrangements.'

Mr Frail wasn't certain what a 'therapeutic regimen' was and normally he would have asked for clarification. He realized, however, that he would be able to ask Pete and that from Pete he was likely to receive an understandable answer. Failing that, he would ask the nurses but he would wait until Dr Backman left the room.

MR FRAIL'S CONFUSION over the multitude of different types of health care workers who would help him recover is common. To the casual observer, it might seem that doctors and nurses provide the bulk of the services offered within the health care system and that all others are only peripheral. The truth is that the specialized services offered by a host of other 'hands-on' health professionals are often essential to the recovery of the patient. Understanding what these people do is key to being a smart patient, which, of course, means knowing the right questions to ask and getting the most out of the specialized services these professionals have to offer. Even though these professionals are rarely your first line of enquiry as you enter the health care system, they are extremely valuable as you progress.

The word 'therapy' is derived from the Greek *therapeia* which means 'service done to the sick.' According to *Dorland's Illustrated Medical Dictionary*, therapy is the 'treatment of disease' (Dorland's 1965, 1570). Although doctors can be classified as therapists under certain conditions, we see them (and they see themselves, make no mistake) as quite separate from the allied health workers who provide unique therapeutic services. Doctors are heavily involved in the process of diagnosis – trying to figure out what the problem is – and therapists, by definition, are primarily concerned with treating the identified problem. It is true that observations made by therapists are often useful in diagnosing health problems, however, their main role is the treatment of disease.

There are many health care workers who provide these specialized kinds of therapy, and they are educated and trained in those specific areas. Let's examine who they are and what they do. Then we'll discuss how you can be a smart patient when you are dealing with them and their services.

A confusion of professional titles

A quick look at any book devoted to helping people choose careers in the health professions is a good way to see the reason for the confusion that exists around professional titles. You are faced by a seemingly endless variety of professionals, all of whom have very specific services to offer. Choosing the right kind of therapist for your particular problem can mean the difference between solving your health problem, learning to adapt to it, or, without such assistance, settling for living in misery.

There are specialized therapeutic services offered in such a wide variety of areas that it would be impossible to discuss every one in a single chapter. Our intention is not to provide exhaustive lists of people and services, but to provide you with an overall way to look at the services that may be available to you. To assist you in wading through this quagmire, we've chosen a few key areas to help you navigate.

You would think that with all the emphasis of North American society on diet and nutrition, everyone would understand the health professionals who provide services in this area. The problem is that there seem to be endless numbers of people who set themselves up as nutritional specialists. These people can range from the highly hyped television personality to the owner of the local health food store. Unfortunately, not everyone who claims to be a nutrition professional can actually use that title with any credibility.

While some of these professionals may have some background and training in nutrition, the only nutrition professionals recognized by mainstream health care are those who have spent four years studying nutrition in an accredited university program. (We'll look at some of the alternatives in chapter 6.) Beyond that, some graduates of these nutrition programs choose to become dietitians, the nutrition specialists you see in hospitals. Those interested individuals who have answered advertisements in the backs of popular health magazines enticing them to become nutrition 'professionals' are not the same as those who have spent years of legitimate study in the areas of food and human nutrition.

Dietitians spend an internship year in a hospital following their graduation from the nutrition degree programs, and they are responsible for nutritional counselling as well as the supervision of hospital food operations. They develop the therapeutic menus. For example, if you are in hospital and your doctor prescribes a diabetic diet for you, the dietitian will design it and teach you how to follow it.

Mr Frail's confusion over the work of the podiatrist is not uncommon. The terms *podiatry* and *chiropractic* are often confused. Podiatrists treat common foot disorders (you may be familiar with the term *chiropody* which is used in Great Britain). They use corrective devices, simple surgical procedures, and orthopaedic shoes. They are trained in approved podiatry colleges and are called 'doctor of podiatry.' Podiatrists are usually not medical doctors, that is, they have not graduated from a medical school.

Chiropractors, whose expertise lies in a completely different area, manipulate the spine and other joints to correct partial and complete dislocations. They focus on avoiding the use of drugs.

Some mainstream doctors still consider chiropractic medicine to be on the fringe. Nevertheless, it is sufficiently mainstream today to discuss it among the accepted allied health care workers, and we therefore include chiropractors here rather than in our discussion of alternate medicine. There are, however, applications of chiropractic medicine that are less mainstream, such as the treatment of babies. Chiropractors graduate from approved colleges of chiropractic medicine and are called 'doctor of chiropractic medicine.' Like podiatrists, chiropractors are not medical doctors.

Somewhat related to the work of the chiropractor in some people's minds is the work of the physiotherapist (or physical therapist). Physiotherapists work to restore function, relieve pain, and prevent disability from a number of conditions. These conditions may develop as a result of a disease or an accident. For example, an individual who suffers a stroke and is paralysed on one side of the body may be able to recover some use of that part of the body by following a regime of physical therapy. Physiotherapists use such physical agents as light, heat, cold, water, and electricity, as well as a variety of mechanical devices such as traction and weights. A physiotherapist has graduated from a four-year professional degree program in a university, with considerable time spent in a hospital or clinic learning clinical procedures and working with actual patients.

Eye care is another area where there are several different categories of workers. The ophthalmologist is the medical doctor specializing in medical and surgical treatment of eye diseases, but there are others who provide much of the care. Opticians are responsible for the actual design and fitting of corrective lenses, and optometrists test eyes and write prescriptions for those lenses (ophthalmologists do this, too). In a strict sense, then, optometrists, whose work appears to be primarily diagnostic, do not clearly fall into our therapeutic category, but they certainly are hands-on health professionals. Optometrists graduate from recognized four-year programs in optometry colleges, usually after two years in university in preparation. They are entitled to be called 'doctors of optometry.' Again, like chiropractors and podiatrists, optometrists are not medical doctors.

Occupational therapy is a health field that is frequently misunderstood. Occupational therapists help people to reach their highest level of independent functioning. They do this by providing ways to overcome problems resulting from physical injury, birth defects, and aging. For example, an occupational therapist might design a piece of equipment for a person who has suffered a stroke so that that person may feed him or herself independently, if using a normal spoon is impossible. They also work with people with diminished levels of functioning resulting from emotional problems. Historically, the stereotypical image of an occupational therapist is that of a worker who teaches basket weaving and other handiwork to psychiatric patients. Although occupational therapists often do work together with psychiatrists, their work is considerably more complex than this incorrect image would lead you to believe. Training in occupational therapy involves a professional university degree program of four or more years which, like all other recognized schools of study in the health professions, requires clinical work during training.

Most people are familiar with the work of pharmacists. Every time you pass by the pharmacy counter in your neighbourhood drugstore on your way to buy shampoo or toothpaste, you can see pharmacists and pharmacy technicians toiling away. Few people have never had to have a doctor's prescription for a drug preparation filled. Thus, the drug-dispensing role of the pharmacist is high profile. What you may not realize is that the work of the pharmacist is much more than counting pills into jars and running retail pharmacy outlets. Today, it is more likely that the person actually counting the pills is a pharmacy technician rather than a professional pharmacist.

The four-year undergraduate university training of a professional pharmacist devotes much time to the study of biochemistry and the intricacies of how drug preparations affect the human body. In addition, recently, pharmacists have taken on a more active role in counselling patients about their prescribed drugs as well as those drugs bought 'over the counter.' What this means is that you are likely to receive a good dose of instruction from your local pharmacist along with your prescription. Your pharmacist probably has more detailed and relevant information about both your prescription and about over-the-counter drugs than your doctor does. This is the person to whom you should direct many of your questions.

Some of the questions you might ask your pharmacist include:

- How do I take this medication (for example, with meals, with milk, under the tongue, by swallowing; how to use a cream)?
- When is the best time for me to take this medication (in the morning, at night, between meals)?
- Am I likely to experience any side effects?
- Are there any other preparations, either prescription or over-the-counter, that I should avoid while on this medication?
- How long do I have to continue taking this?
- Can I have it refilled without seeing my doctor again?
- Are there any precautions I need to consider while on this medication (like avoiding sun exposure, or not operating a car or other equipment)?

Although your doctor may have given you much of this information when writing the prescription, this is the time to ensure that you understand it. The answers to these questions are also important when you select your own over-the-counter medications without consulting your doctor. In this situation, you need your pharmacist even more.

Another group of people providing important, specialized allied health services are those whose work focuses on hearing and speech. These specialists are audiologists and speech pathologists. Their role in the diagnosis of particular problems may be among the largest of the allied health professionals in diagnosis.

An audiologist both tests hearing and works to assist the person with a hearing problem to cope with it. The speech pathologist (sometimes called a speech therapist) tests and diagnoses speech problems and designs therapy programs to solve them. A child who stutters, for example, may be referred to a speech pathologist for treatment. Often people tend to think of these health professionals not as part of health care but of education. This is because hearing and speech professionals are often employed by school boards. They are, however, very important parts of the health care system.

And there are other therapists. The number of specialty areas that are currently used therapeutically has increased dramatically over the past twenty years. Even though this is not meant to be an exhaustive discussion of therapeutic avenues, it is worth mentioning some of the more high profile jobs. Some more recent additions to the therapeutic arsenal are art therapy, music therapy, dance and movement therapy, and recreational therapy. Before using the services of such individuals, it is important to ensure that they have acceptable credentials. It isn't enough to be a music teacher and decide to become a music therapist. These therapists also study their specialty, although the courses of study can vary. Research these people carefully before embarking on a course of treatment with them. One way to begin this research is to contact a professional association such as those listed in the back of this book. These organizations can provide you with descriptions of what these therapists do and how they are educated and licensed. You may also want to call a nearby university that educates health professionals to find someone who knows about the specialty you are researching. Finally, try to talk to someone who has received treatment from this specialist to get the patient's perspective. If you are computer literate and have access to the Internet and World Wide Web, one of the increasingly popular ways to get information is to post a query on a consumer health network (suggestions for which ones you might try are listed in the back of this book).

Finally, we need to talk about another kind of 'hands-on' health care worker, but one that doesn't really fit into our definition of therapists. This group is one of growing importance in the United States: the physician assistant. Virtually unknown north of the forty-ninth parallel, PAs, as they are called, practise medicine under the supervision of a licensed physician, performing a range of duties from basic primary care to some high-technology specialty procedures. Some of these procedures might include taking medical histories, performing physical examinations, ordering laboratory tests, diagnosing common illnesses, determining treatment, counselling patients, promoting wellness, and assisting in surgery.

Physician assistants receive their education in universities that award them either a bachelor's degree or a certificate of completion, and, in some cases an associate or master's degree. Most educational programs require PA students to have a minimum of two years of university preparation before they are admitted. Once in the PA program, students study subjects that resemble the curriculum of a traditional medical school, including anatomy, physiology, pharmacology, microbiology, ethics, family medicine, internal medicine, and emergency medicine. In addition to the coursework that generally makes up the first year of the program, students complete a year of clinical placements. At the end of two calendar years, the PA graduates. A physician assistant who has graduated from an accredited school and taken a national certifying examination can use the title 'physician assistant–certified (PA-C).'

In the United States, you may find that your doctor or clinic employs physician assistants in a variety of ways. You may find the PA doing all routine examinations, giving needles to your children, and teaching you about your medications, all under the supervision of a doctor.

There seems little interest in Canada at present to develop this level of medical care, in spite of the widely discussed regional shortage of doctors, a situation that the position of physician assistant was developed to address in the United States in the 1960s.

Finding your way out of the maze

Obviously, as a smart patient, you will want to be able to use the services of the most appropriate health professional to deal with your problem. If you have a solid relationship with a family doctor whom you trust and whose values you share, you will be able to use this person as your conduit to other avenues of treatment. Keep in mind that often the catalyst for your referral to these therapists will be a doctor, anyway.

If your doctor refers you to another type of therapist, ensure that you understand exactly what that person's role in your care will be and how your doctor and the therapist will communicate with each other. Ask both the doctor who refers you and the therapist the expected outcomes for the course of treatment. Often it is preferable to leave the coordination of your care to your family doctor, as he or she is the most likely of the health professionals to have broader information about your health status.

Read the available written information (you may need to contact some of the professional associations that we list in the back of this book) about the type of treatment you will receive. A word of caution: be careful how you interpret what you read in the popular press. If your favourite magazine has just written an article about this type of therapy, its slant on it may reflect more its own point of view than any objective description of the topic. This applies equally to those articles that support and those that detract from the therapy discussed. When you approach health professionals to ask questions that have been generated by the media, be careful how you word them. Try to avoid being accusatory in any way. Don't imply that you believe everything that you read. Let the health professional you are asking give you his or her answer without putting that person on the defensive. You are more likely to get an honest and useful response.

Some of these health professionals discussed here will be self-employed, and others will be employed by a hospital or clinic. Those who are self-employed are not only health professionals but business people as well. Although this may have little direct impact on their actual patient services, it will have an impact on how the services may be organized. A physiotherapist who works for a hospital out-patient department, for example, will have different constraints than one who is self-employed. For one thing, a therapist who is self-employed needs to be concerned about both patient care and the bottom line. This has both positive and what would seem like negative effects. On the positive side, from

your point of view, the competition among self-employed professionals for patients may result in nice service perks, and you
can shop around for those perks that most appeal to you. On the
other hand, there may be more concern about appointment scheduling and ensuring that each patient receives only his or her
allotted time.

Try to develop a relationship with the professional treating
you. Your therapist is likely to want a good relationship with
you anyway, but you can make it more useful to you if you take
on an active role here. Don't just play the subservient patient.
The service you are offered may be very important to you, but
you are also important and your role in achieving a successful
outcome is not a small one.

Therapists come in all shapes, sizes, and specialties. This can
be one of the most confusing categories of health professionals to
sort out because you may have to do it almost all by yourself. If
you have already developed a good relationship with your primary caregiver, your family doctor, then you will be able to consult with him or her about finding an appropriate therapist. As a
smart patient you will then begin to see that finding the right
health professional for the right job results in better care for you.
Don't expect your family doctor to be able to provide all the care
your family needs.

6

The Alternatives

Of all the mistakes made by physicians and the medical world that hurt the American people, one of the most powerful and pervasive is their erroneous belief that they alone practice medicine.

Charles Inlander, Lowell Levin, and Ed Weiner, *Medicine on Trial*,

p. 154

As soon as Emily Aaron walked through his door carrying a big bouquet of wild flowers and a basket of his favourite fruit, Mr Frail could feel a smile erupt all the way down from the top of his head to the bottom of his toes. Emily was just about his best friend in the whole world.

A 67-year-old widow, Emily was also a bona fide eccentric, and Mr Frail loved her for it. She was his neighbour in the apartment building where he had lived alone since his wife died ten years earlier. The flowing Indian print skirt topped with a linen sweater disguised the painful arthritis that Emily fought continually. But she had her ways of coping with it.

Emily had visited Mr Frail once a week since his hospital admission, and the nurses had learned enough about the couple in that time to warn Mr Frail if they saw his daughter coming down the hall while Emily was there. His daughter disapproved heartily of his relationship with Emily and made no secret of her opinion. But Emily's presence did more for Mr Frail than just about anything the doctors could do to make him feel better.

'Norman, my dear, you are looking so much better today,' said Emily as she embraced him warmly.

'And now I'm feeling much better, too,' he beamed. Emily always managed to make him feel like a 16-year-old, inside anyway.

'As soon as you're out of the clutches of the health care system, I'm going to get my caregiver over to see you.' Emily busied herself with taking fruit out of the basket and arranging the flowers on the bedside table.

'Just exactly what kind of *caregiver* did you have in mind?' Mr Frail had been through this before with Emily, and, although he was somewhat open-minded in discussing the issue with Emily, it inevitably ended up with him having a heated argument with his daughter who was, to his mind, somewhat closed-minded.

'You know that Chinese medicine specialist I've been seeing for my arthritis? Well, I told her about you, and she said she would be glad to see you.'

'Emily, you know that I'd be willing to give some things a try, but I've seen those concoctions you've been brewing up on the stove. That stuff looks like you picked it up off the ground in the park. And it smells vile.'

Emily laughed. Mr Frail had often been in her apartment when she had been cooking up her herbal tea. She made it from a special prescription mixture of herbs and roots that she mail-ordered from Toronto. In truth, the concoction did smell revolting and tasted worse, but as far as she was concerned, the tea and the acupuncture treatments she took weekly were keeping her arthritis under control.

Dr Backman and Pete opened the door and came in quickly, as Dr Backman always did.

'Mr Frail,' Dr Backman began. 'We're getting ready to discharge you.' At that, Emily clapped her hands and smiled widely. Dr Backman hardly looked at her before continuing.

'Dr Kowalski will write out your prescriptions and attend to the physiotherapy appointments necessary for your full recovery. I'll drop by just before you leave.' And he was gone, without even examining him. Pete stayed behind.

'Poison and torture!' said Emily.

Pete looked at her, puzzled.

'Drugs and physiotherapy,' she said, 'poison and torture.'

Pete had already had the pleasure of meeting Emily on several earlier occasions, and Mr Frail had filled him in about her – so, too, had Mr Frail's daughter, and the stories were quite different from one another.

'Pete, Emily says that I should see her Chinese doctor for those herbs and acupuncture. What do you think?'

Pete didn't think he wanted to get into this at all. 'Well, Mr Frail, I don't really know much about herbs. I do know a little about acupuncture.'

'There, see, these doctors don't even know about alternative types of medical treatment,' Emily said. 'They don't even teach you about it in medical school today, do they?'

Pete shrugged. 'I guess since that's not what they're training us to do, they figure it shouldn't be part of the curriculum. All I know is that some people seem to have good effects from some of the alternative approaches, but I'd be careful. Most of the forms of treatment are unregulated, and anyone can say that she knows what she's doing. I just don't feel comfortable with it all.'

'At least he's honest, Em,' Mr Frail said. 'And a bit open-minded, which is more than I can say for my daughter, as you well know.'

Emily nodded.

'Just be careful, Mr Frail. We're going to prescribe a treatment regimen that we know is likely to have a good effect on you and help you recover to the fullest extent possible. If you want to try some other approaches, that's your choice, but I wouldn't expect too much, and they might even make you sicker. I'll come back later to explain it to you.'

PETE'S DISCOMFORT at discussing the efficacy of alternative forms of health treatment is not unexpected. As public interest in alternative forms of medical treatment has increased, mainstream medicine has become increasingly uncomfortable with it and, to some people's minds, somewhat defensive.

This increased interest in alternative ways of regaining and maintaining health is attributable at least in part to a growing mistrust of mainstream medicine. When viewing mainstream medicine, many people see what appears to be a headlong rush toward invasive interventions such as surgery or drug therapy, fuelled by the profit orientation of large pharmaceutical companies. Regardless of the reason for the upswing in interest, alternative forms of medical care are among the choices that you have today in health care. As a smart patient, you need to know a bit about what you are buying in this realm as well. And buying you are.

Whether your health care is paid for by a health insurance plan administered by a government body (as for most Canadians and some Americans) or by a private insurer, alternative approaches to medical care are not often covered. For instance, you may find that acupuncture used by a licensed physician or physiotherapist is covered, but other types of treatment or those provided by unregulated caregivers probably are not. This is an issue you may wish to check on, as even alternative forms of treatment can be expensive.

Let's start by looking at the approaches that mainstream medicine considers 'alternative medicine' and then discuss how you can be a smart patient when it comes to including or not including them in your own health care regimen.

What makes something alternative

An alternative is something that is used in place of something else. By definition it does not imply that one of the choices is inherently better than the other. Indeed, the implication is that one can be used to replace the other. Whether this is true depends on your point of view.

When we discuss alternative medicine, we're usually referring to approaches to health and medical care that are not generally enshrined in our health care system. The approaches that fall into this category are defined by society. For example, acupuncture for pain control provided by a physician or physiotherapist is usually considered to be mainstream today, whereas acupuncture provided by a traditional Chinese medical practitioner for liver dysfunction is not. For other 'alternative' approaches, the line between mainstream and alternative is clearer.

Another term that is gaining in popularity to describe these alternative approaches is *complementary medicine*. Complementary has a different meaning than alternative. An alternative is something used in place of something else. According to Webster's Dictionary, complementary, means 'helping to constitute a whole or to supply a lack ... mutually providing each other's needs' (Webster's 1993, 206). This seems like a much more cooperative way of looking at mainstream and alternative medicine. It implies that one approach fits in with the other. As comforting as this thought may be to those who espouse choices in health care, as we do, in reality there is still considerable animosity between those who practise 'traditional' medicine in North America, as currently taught in our medical schools, and those who practise 'alternative' medicine, as highlighted by the quote at the beginning of this chapter.

Organized medicine in North America has a long history of suspicion of anything it considers to be on the fringe. Alternative medicine falls into that category, and today's average physician is not known for open-mindedness about alternatives. One of the main reasons cited by doctors and organized medicine for this disdain is what they see as the untested nature of alternative approaches. Notwithstanding the frequent lack of scientific rigour in assessing mainstream medical approaches, it is true that many alternative approaches have not been scientifically tested either for efficacy or for safety. The practitioners rely on anecdotal information about the results.

One of the most important concerns that you as a patient should consider is that most alternative approaches to health and medical care are unlicensed and thus unregulated. The training of these caregivers can vary enormously, and a smart patient will investigate a caregiver's background. For example, there are no regulations governing the practice of herbalism, thus, anyone can study the use of herbs in health and illness and set up a consultancy in the field. The real problem here is that herbal treatments, and other similar approaches to alternative health care, are not without their dangers. Lack of regulation can be problematic if the patient doesn't use the 'buyer beware' approach to selecting alternatives (see our discussion of how to evaluate backgrounds of alternative health care providers later in this chapter).

A sampling of alternatives

We can't provide you with an exhaustive list and discussion of all the alternative approaches to medical care that are available in North America today. We probably don't even know what they all are! What we can do, however, is discuss some of the most common and high profile of these approaches, ones that you may seriously consider using.

Midwifery
Midwives have been around at least since biblical times. Their job is to provide care to women during pregnancy and childbirth. We start with midwifery as it is the one alternative approach that is closest to being a part of mainstream medicine today. Midwifery is licensed in several Canadian provinces. Although the practice differs widely throughout the world, North American midwifery represents an alternative to modern obstetrical care. The focus of the midwife is on the normal, natural aspects of pregnancy and childbirth and, to a large extent, on the psychological aspects of the experience for the family. Midwives have a distinctly low tech approach. Some practice in conjunction with hospitals and obstetricians; others are independent. Their training can also vary.

Acupuncture
At least in a limited way, acupuncture, too, has made its way into mainstream medicine. Developed by the Chinese, it is a centuries-old approach to treating a whole host of dysfunctions. Acupuncture involves inserting thin, solid needles into specific points on the body. Acupuncturists vary with regard to their background, experience, and philosophy. A growing

concern among consumers of acupuncture today is the HIV–AIDS situation. The procedure should be done only with pre-packaged, sterilized, disposable needles that are used only once.

Homeopathy

Developed in the early nineteenth century, homeopathy flourished for a long time before falling into disrepute in the twentieth century, only to experience a recent resurgence. It is based on the belief that symptoms of a disease are evidence of a curative process of the body in response to the disease, like the fever that you get in response to a viral infection. The increase in body temperature provides the virus with an environment that is not conducive to its continued growth. Homeopathic doctors give the patient drugs that further induce those symptoms in an attempt to boost that curative, natural response of the body. Even though it might seem that this could actually be disastrous for the patient – to experience even worse symptoms – one of the principles of homeopathic medicine is that the smaller the dose, the more effective the drug. In this way, the drugs are rendered essentially harmless. There are schools of homeopathic medicine throughout North America.

Herbalism

Herbalism is the practice of using various roots and herbs for their medicinal qualities. A practitioner of herbalism prescribes a specific mixture to treat a specific condition. The herbs and roots are usually boiled into a tea (although there is a considerable market in prepared, packaged herbs in capsules). Knowledge of the effects of these herbal remedies is largely anecdotal, passed on through generations. Herbalists have a wide variety of backgrounds and include both those who are self-taught and those who have received some instruction.

Massage Therapy

Developed by the Chinese, massage therapy and related manipulation has been used for centuries. Modern physiotherapists also use massage.

Traditional Chinese Medicine

Deeply rooted in the Chinese view of the universe, traditional Chinese medicine is an ancient practice. It has, however, become an increasingly popular form of alternative treatment in North America. Practitioners of TCM in North America are often educated in schools of Chinese medicine throughout the continent, primarily in the United States.

TCM uses a number of the techniques that we have already discussed. These include acupuncture, herbal treatments, and a technique called moxibustion which involves burning 'moxa,' a combustible substance, on the surface of the skin in specific areas, much like those chosen for acupuncture.

The 30 per cent solution

The modern, scientific medical community looks on these approaches with a not-too-well-hidden scepticism, and practitioners of alternative medicine continue to use mainly anecdotal evidence to support their claims. We don't want to appear judgmental in any way, and both of us have sought out and undergone acupuncture, herbal treatments, and moxibustion at one time or another, so we definitely fall into the category of being open-minded. Nevertheless, it is worth bearing in mind that one of the ways that modern medicine explains the successes of some of these approaches is with what we call the 30 per cent solution, otherwise known as the 'placebo effect.'

A placebo is a harmless substance that the patient believes is a treatment. It is widely known in the medical field that if you give ten patients a placebo, sugar pills, for example, which they believe to be a painkiller, you can predict with statistical accuracy that three of those people will actually experience relief from their pain. This 'placebo effect' is the result of the powerful influence our brains have on our bodies. If we believe something strongly enough, this belief can have actual physical effects.

Often when we seek alternative approaches to healing, it is the result of a futile attempt to find relief for our problem in mainstream medicine, where the search typically begins. It may be because the particular problem is intractable, and modern medicine fails even to recognize it as a 'real' medical problem. This is currently the case with such ailments as chronic fatigue syndrome and even with environmental illnesses. Thus, we seek another form of treatment. A belief in the effectiveness of a medical treatment often has a profoundly positive effect on the outcome for an average of 30 per cent of patients so treated. Their testimonials may seen too impressive to ignore.

The smart alternative consumer

When it comes to being a smart patient, it's just as important when dealing with alternative approaches to health care.

First, it's important for you to research the approach you want to try before bringing it up with your family doctor. Given the disdain with which most doctors in North America treat alternative approaches, your own firm footing regarding information will at least help. But do discuss it with your doctor. This doesn't mean that you necessarily will follow your family doctor's advice, but your primary caregiver should know that you are doing this.

Check the credentials of the person who will treat you. Find out where and when the individual trained and how much experience he or she has. The best way to do this is to set up an appointment for you to interview the prospective caregiver. You'll probably have to pay for this, but it may be a small price for finding out that this person should or should not treat you.

If at all possible, get a recommendation from someone who has actually been treated by that person. If you have a friend or relative whose judgment you trust, ask some questions. If you get to the caregiver's place of business and you don't like what you experience, leave. If the office doesn't appear clean or businesslike, and you are uncomfortable, don't feel obliged to go through with treatment.

The bottom line is that this is a choice available to you, but be careful.

Alternative approaches to medical care are gaining in popularity with the North American patient. If you have never sought out an alternative practitioner yourself, you probably know people who have. As time passes, however, there is likely to be more, rather than less, interest in these approaches. Indeed, there are moves in many areas to regulate and further develop some of them. As a smart patient, you will ensure that you know as much about these alternatives as you can, so that you maintain your choices in health care.

PART 2
THE PROCESS

Now that you have become more familiar with your doctor and others who provide health care services, the question is: what processes allow these people to do their jobs for you? Health professionals use techniques and approaches that include diagnostic tests, drugs, high tech equipment, and surgical procedures. We'll take you behind the scenes to see how these processes work, and we'll look at how you can use them and then get a second opinion. But before we do that, we want you to be privy to some of the secret 'in-talk' of real doctors, nurses, and other health professionals.

7
Medical Buzztalk

I know professors in this country who 'ligate' arteries. Other surgeons
only tie them, and it stops the bleeding just as well.

Oliver Wendell Holmes (1809–94)
Medical Essays

When Eleanor Gass stepped onto the elevator the next morning
to follow up on the arrangements for her father's discharge, she
was not a happy woman. Insisting that he wished to maintain
some independence from his family, her father, Mr Frail, had
instructed her to find him a temporary bed in a rehabilitation
facility of some sort. She had fully expected to take him home
with her and hire some help. Now she had been obliged to find
him a temporary bed in a long-term care facility where he could
recover sufficiently to go home to his own apartment, not to her
home.

She had spent the past two days scouring the area for such a
facility, and, furthermore, she fully believed that this would make
her life even more miserable than it already was. Instead of simply going upstairs to see her father, she would now have to take
a half-hour drive out into the country, because that was the location of the closest facility with an available bed. To the casual
observer, Eleanor Gass looked like she was sucking on a pickle
when the elevator stopped on the second floor, and a group of
chattering doctor-types got on.

'That was the slickest ET tube I've seen you pass yet,' one of the white-coated young men said to a white-coated young woman.

'Yeah. For a minute there I thought I'd have some trouble. You know he had some stenosis that hadn't been apparent previously. It just seemed to be one thing after the other. When you started to push that bolus of lidocaine and the respiratory tech bumped into you, I though you were going to slap an IV in *him*!'

'Do they always go from V-Tach to asystole when you use 400 joules?' This question came from the young man who appeared to be the most junior. He seemed in awe of everything the others said and did.

The most senior young man laughed. 'You never know what'll happen during a code.'

Just then three pocket pagers began bleeping alarmingly. They all looked at their belts to see the numbers flashing across the tiny read-out. 'It's another code, seventh floor.'

The doors opened and they all rushed out as if *their* lives depended on it. Eleanor was left wondering what the heck they had been talking about.

IF YOU'VE EVER WATCHED A TELEVISION MEDICAL DRAMA, you've probably heard a lot of it before. You know, the emergency medical technicians rush through the ER doors pushing some poor soul on a stretcher. Then, they begin yelling to one another, 'Knife wound, right upper quadrant; sinus tachycardia; BP 90 over 50 and falling.' Then a doctor rushes onto the scene. 'Start another IV of Ringer's at 120 cc an hour. We need a CBC stat. Group and cross him for six units, stat. Get surgery down here, stat.'

The amazing thing is that you probably understand most of that medical jargon just from watching TV. What they really said is that the patient has a knife wound somewhere in the vicinity of his liver, his heart is beating rapidly, and his blood pressure is falling (all of which indicate that he is probably going into shock as a result of blood loss). The doctor wants another intravenous line with a particular solution to run into the patient at a drip rate of 120 cc per hour. She also wants a complete blood count done and she wants to ensure that there will be six units of matched blood available for this patient should he need it. And she wants all of this 'stat' which, of course, means immediately.

If you were able to figure most of that out, don't start patting yourself on the back for your ability to understand the language of medicine. Most of the medical buzztalk that your doctor never lets you in on is far more mundane than the dramatic scene in the emergency room. It is, however, likely to be considerably more important to your understanding of your health care. If you can't even understand the words that your doctor is using to explain something to you, you immediately begin to lose control of your health care. Understanding what we have termed *medical buzztalk* is key to taking and keeping control of your health care experience.

Let's peek into another office at the hospital where a doctor is just explaining a procedure to a patient so that the patient will sign a consent form. Here is what the doctor is saying to the patient:

'It seems you have quite severe myocardial insufficiency. I want you to have a cardiac cath – You've no doubt heard of a cardiac cath. We do them all the time – We'll be inserting a catheter into your femoral artery and passing it through your abdominal aorta to your heart. When it reaches your heart, we'll inject a radiopaque dye through the catheter so that we'll be able to visualize clearly the areas of stenosis – There is a small risk that the catheter could irritate the electrical conduction system of your heart as it passes through, setting off an arrhythmia, but that's unlikely – Any questions?'

Huh??

Of course, the obvious answer here is for the patient to begin asking the doctor specific questions for clarification. The problem is that, in these circumstances, it is often difficult to know where to start. What we would like to do is give you that starting point.

There are three aspects to developing an understanding of this medical buzztalk. First, as you have seen, there is the actual medical terminology. It isn't our intention to provide you with a course on medical terminology. Nevertheless, we would like to give you a starting point for understanding terms. Second, hospitals and medical personnel use a wide variety of abbreviations in their written communication. We have gathered some of the most common ones so that when you have your own medical record or a consult you are hand-delivering to your consultant from your family doctor, you may understand some of these abbreviations. Finally, we come to the most interesting and sometimes alarming aspect of medical buzztalk: the use of what we politely call colloquialisms. These are unofficial terms that evolve in the speech patterns of doctors and other health care workers that they use only when they are talking to each other. We'll let you in on a few.

Real medical terminology

Years ago, any young student who aspired to a career in medicine was required to pursue the study of Latin in preparation for medical school. Many of us had that experience. It might seem that only historians ought to be interested in a dead language – one that no one in the world actually speaks any more – but the fact that it also provides a basis for much of the English language makes it of interest, especially to linguists. Why is it of interest to doctors?

The reason is that much medical terminology has its roots in Latin and also in Greek. Understanding these languages helps us to decipher specific medical terms that we use in English. For example, the term 'cardiac' which refers to the heart, is derived from the Latin *cardiacus* which is derived from the Greek *kardiakos*, which, of course, means heart. Or, the Greek word for kidney is *nephros*, and Greek for excision is *ektome*. Putting these together gives you the word 'nephrectomy,' which means excision or removal of the kidney. By the way, the term 'stat,' which seems to be favourite among the television doctor-types, is derived from the Latin *statim*, which means immediately.

Understanding some of the basics of prefixes (the beginnings of words) allows you to figure out what a word generally refers to. Table 7.1 provides a list of some of the common prefixes used in medical terminology. This is by no means an exhaustive re-

Table 7.1
Common Prefixes and Roots in Medical Terminology

ante:	before	mamm:	breast
anti:	against	morph:	shape
arthr:	related to the joints	nephr:	related to the kidney
arter:	related to the arteries	neur:	related to the nerves
brady:	slow	ocul:	related to the eye
bronch:	related to the lower windpipe	odont:	related to the teeth
		ophthalm:	related to the eye
carcin:	related to cancer	orth:	straight
circum:	around	path:	sickness
contra:	against	ped:	child
derm:	related to the skin	peri:	around
enter:	related to the intestine	phag:	eat
gastr:	related to the stomach	pharyng:	related to the throat
gyn:	related to women	phleb:	related to the veins
hepat:	related to the liver	pneum:	related to air, lungs
lapar:	flank	pod:	related to the feet
laryng:	related to the upper windpipe	proct:	related to the anus
		pseud:	false
leuk:	white	pulmo:	related to the lung
lingu:	related to the tongue	rhino:	related to the nose
lith:	stone	sanguin:	related to the blood
lumb:	loin	sten:	narrow
lymph:	water	thorac:	related to the chest

view, but a listing of those we have found in practice to be the most common. To aid you in understanding medical terms, we recommend that you buy yourself and your family a medical dictionary. They are widely available at bookstores throughout North America and, in the back of this book, we recommend several that would be useful in your own collection. When a health care worker uses a word that you don't understand, ask for clarification and the correct spelling. That gives you the opportunity to go to the dictionary at your leisure to increase your understanding.

With the popularity of television medical dramas on the upswing, it seemed a natural progression that education programs such as *Operation*, made available on the public broadcasting systems, should gain something of a cult following. There is a grow-

ing interest in getting behind the scenes in medical care today –
and the more realistic the programs are, the better their viewers
like them. Being able to understand the terminology goes a long
way toward improving your ability to understand the procedures.
These shows are careful to use only correct medical terms that
are vetted by medical consultants. Using our chart, you should
be able to understand what they say in short order!

Acronyms and abbreviations

Just like any field, medicine has its own acronyms and abbreviations. Some, however, are more common than others, thus, of
more interest to the average patient. If you want to be a smart
patient, you will want to learn the meanings of some of these. It
is also true, however, that these can vary by region. You will find
that one abbreviation may mean one thing in one place and another thing in another institution. The abbreviation LOC, for example, can mean both loss of consciousness or level of consciousness, leading to some confusion. Even if abbreviations may not
be the clearest way to communicate, they are part of medical
buzztalk in a big way. Many of the full terms are long and cum-
bersome, thus, these abbreviations allow health professionals to
communicate more efficiently, if not more effectively. They are
used in written communication, and you'll even hear them when
doctors, nurses, and all the others talk to each other! This becomes a particular problem when they lapse into abbreviations
and acronyms when talking to you.

Table 7.2 lists some of the most commonly used medical abbreviations, and table 7.3 provides an explanation for some of the
abbreviations that refer to locations in the hospital. Next time
you have a look at your chart or enter a hospital, check how
many you can see or hear.

Secret 'in' talk

One of the most interesting parts of medical communication is
the use of terms that health professionals employ only when they

Table 7.2
Common Abbreviations in Medical Buzztalk

Abbreviation	Stands for ...	Refers to ...
BPR	bleeding per rectum	blood coming from the rectum
BRP	bathroom privileges	a level of activity allowed
CAD	coronary artery disease	disease of the vessels of the heart
CVA	cerebrovascular accident	a stroke
DNR	do not resuscitate	an order for no heroics
ETOH	alcohol	a drinking habit
FUO	fever of unknown origin	a health problem that needs investigation
GERD	gastroesophageal reflux disease	a stomach problem
IHD	ischemic heart disease	narrowing of heart vessels
LOC	loss or level of consciousness	part of an examination
NAD	no abnormality demonstrated	a description of a patient
NKDA	no known drug allergy	the answer to questions asked of every patient
NPO	nothing by mouth	an order given before some tests and operations
NYD	not yet diagnosed	health problems that need investigation
PERLA	pupils equal and reactive to light and accommodation	what happens when a light is shone in the eyes
PPD	packs per day	a cigarette habit
PUO	pyrexia of unknown origin	a health problem that needs investigation
PVD	peripheral vascular disease	disease of other blood vessels
SOBOE	shortness of breath on exertion	trouble breathing
TKVO	to keep vein open	the speed of an IV solution
VSS	vital signs stable	temperature, pulse, and respiration

Table 7.3
Abbreviations of Hospital Locations

CCU	coronary care unit
ER	emergency room
ICU	intensive care unit
NICU	neuro- or neonatal ICU
OR	operating room
RR	recovery room

are talking to each other (and they are usually quite careful about this for reasons that will soon become apparent). You might ask why such patterns of communication develop at all. Is it that medical people want to appear to be 'in the know,' or are they really trying to hide something from you, the patient?

According to two folklore researchers in the United States, sometimes the terminology is, indeed, used to actively conceal information from the patient (George and Dundes 1978). This would be somewhat like a parent spelling out something in front of a young child who knows that the parents are saying something that they do not want the child to understand.

Hospitals sometimes use euphemisms such as 'code' or 'code blue' to announce to the special team that a patient has suffered a cardiac arrest. This is ostensibly to reduce the panic on the part of those who are listening. In the same way, the term 'code red' or 'Dr Red' used over a loudspeaker may mean that there is a fire somewhere in the building. These terms vary considerably from one hospital to another.

One odd acronym that is a part of hospital folk speech is 'FLK.' This stands for 'funny looking kid' and is usually employed only when doctors and nurses are talking to each other, or is written only on something that doesn't become a permanent part of the patient's record. Doctors use it when examining a child who doesn't look quite right but they don't yet know what might be the cause of the problem.

A number of these folk terms are unflattering references to specific types of patients. Our sources within the resident staff of hospitals currently tell us that the term 'shoo buzzard' refers to a terminal patient, usually old and vegetative. These kinds of terms are often used to diffuse the stress and powerlessness physicians can feel when dealing with patients they cannot cure.

Another such term, one that is perhaps more widely used, is the term GOMER. We were first introduced to it in a novel by physician–author Samuel Shem. This piece of fiction, *The House of God*, is an irreverent look at the stresses of being an intern or resident in modern medical training; it enjoyed something of a cult following among hospital house staff when it was published.

There is some controversy about the origin of GOMER. It fairly consistently, however, refers to a patient who is old, unkempt, often alcoholic, and possessed of numerous intractable, chronic conditions. This pretty well describes everything that is anathema to the modern attempt to cure, cure, cure. Some people believe that it stands for 'Get Out of My Emergency Room,' which can be interpreted to mean that acute-care physicians and nurses who work in such high-stress areas as emergency departments might not be interested in caring for such chronic problems as presented by the old, unkempt, and alcoholic-type patient. Another interpretation is that GOMER stands for 'Grand Old Man of the Emergency Room,' a distinctly more flattering explanation than the previous one. There does, however, seem to be some agreement that the term applies only to men (George and Dundes 1978).

If you were to do a survey of the house staff (interns and residents) in a large teaching hospital, you would likely uncover more terms such as FLK, shoo-buzzard, and GOMER that may be used regionally. You might be severely offended by such derisive terms in reference to patients, but keep in mind that their use is usually not malicious. It can, however, be an extremely unpleasant occurrence when you recognize such terms, and they are being used by doctors and nurses within earshot of you or your loved ones. If medical personnel are going to continue to use these terms, it should not be at your expense or that of your family. Should you hear such terms, you should discuss this with the nurse and physician in charge. We don't propose attempting to stop doctors and nurses from employing such terms when they are talking among themselves, but no patient should ever be subjected to hearing them.

Just like the legalese used by lawyers and the financial jargon so popular among accountants, doctors have their own terminology. This comes as no surprise to you. It only stands to reason that there must be names for all those unpleasant medical conditions, not to mention every part of the body. What smart patients know, however, is that doctors also use acronyms and colloquialisms that they don't necessarily intend for you to understand. Ask when you fail to understand some of the medical buzztalk.

8
Tests, Tests, and More Tests

Eleanor followed slowly behind the rushing crowd of doctors from the elevator on the seventh floor. On her route to her father's room she passed through another nursing unit where the nurses were having their 3 p.m. 'report.' Eleanor had been around hospitals enough over the years to know what that meant. It would be unlikely that she would see a nurse for anything at all for the next half hour. This was the time where the nurses just going off duty sit down with the nurses just arriving to tell them what's been happening. As Eleanor stopped at the water fountain, she heard bits and pieces of their conversation.

'Room 728 bed one, Mrs Avery, age 45, gallstones. She's scheduled for a cholecystectomy on Monday but she needs a cardiac work-up. There's a requisition on her chart for an ECG and echocardiogram. Then they'll decide on a stress test. Her blood work needs to be set out, too. She needs a CBC and diff and a SMAC. Also, set her up for a urinalysis in the morning.'

'Room 728, bed two, Mrs Chan, age 52, abdominal pain NYD. She's having a laparoscopic in the morning. Most of her blood work is back, and the results of her CT scan are on her chart. Get the resident to have a look at that tonight, will you? They've been awfully busy today.'

'Room 728, bed three, Mrs Constable, age 74, mastectomy. We sent cultures on her drainage this morning. She still has to have those irrigations three times a day. It's looking better, but the incision is still infected.'

Eleanor didn't want to hear any more (not that she under-stood most of it anyway). She had often wished she had gone to nursing school, but her life had led her in a totally different direction as a newspaper reporter. Now, nurses and doctors seemed to live in their own private world and speak a language few others understood. What the heck were all those tests any-way? She briefly wondered if the patients really needed all of them. She'd have to look into that some time – it might make a good story. Now, it was time to head to her father's nursing unit to try to find a nurse to talk to.

As Eleanor rounded the corner she found no one at the nurs-ing station, which wasn't that unusual. But she also noticed a gathering of people in the hallway outside her father's doorway. She remembered the page the cardiac arrest team had received in the elevator, and an unaccustomed panic began to rise within her.

Eleanor quickened her pace as she began to pick up snippets of conversation. She saw young Dr Pete Kowalski standing out-side the door.

When he looked up from the notebook in his hand, he began walking toward her.

'Mrs Gass,' he began, 'your father has just had a bit of a prob-lem.'

'A cardiac arrest?' she asked numbly.

'Actually, yes.' Pete saw the look on her face and added quickly, 'But he's okay now.'

'How okay is a man his age after his heart has stopped beating?'

'Well, his heart is beating well now, and he's awake. I'll check and see if it's okay for you to see him.'

Pete had been just as shocked as Eleanor when he walked onto the unit and saw the cardiac arrest team with the defibrillator rushing into Mr Frail's room. He had felt a lump in his throat, and he had begun to walk more quickly. As the intern on orthopaedics, however, despite the fact that Mr Frail was one of his patients, Pete had little responsibility in this situation. The cardiac arrest team would do its job.

As Pete ushered Eleanor in to see her father, the cardiology resident was rhyming off a list of tests he wanted Mr Frail to have – ECG, cardiac enzymes, echocardiogram ... Mr Frail wouldn't be going home today.

THE WORD 'DIAGNOSIS' comes from the Greek *gnosis*, which means knowledge, and in medicine it means the art (and increasingly the science) of distinguishing one disease from another. Even though much information can be gathered clinically from observations of the patient's symptoms, and can result in what is called a clinical diagnosis (which is largely how simple, well-understood conditions are diagnosed), without assistance the doctor cannot know much of what is happening inside the body. In medicine today, that assistance comes from an arsenal of diagnostic tests. You may not be aware that there are literally hundreds of different tests that modern medicine has to offer. An old medical dictionary has a list of tests that are contained in no fewer than forty-three double-columned pages!

As a patient, you are fortunate, indeed, that your doctor has access to such a wonderful variety of ways of seeing inside your body. Early in the century, the physician had no way to look at what was inside the body, either physically or chemically, and thus no way to determine the root cause of many of the symptoms presented by patients. Modern diagnostic tests have greatly improved our understanding of how disease processes work internally.

As a smart patient, however, you need to be armed with information so that you can do a number of things:

- understand the doctor's explanation of the need for tests
- ask further questions about the tests themselves and the reasons for them
- have input into the decision that enough tests have been done

Success and safety in diagnostic testing

Success and safety are two very important issues when it comes to procedures that affect your health in any way. When it comes to diagnostic testing, it is important to ask two questions:

- How likely is this test to be successful in finding out what's wrong with me?
- What are the risks involved in undergoing this test?

Let's look first at the issue of success in testing.

No doubt most of you have heard stories of false positive results in diagnostic testing. The media coverage of false positives in HIV testing has been particularly dramatic. If you believe that you have any disease, it is likely to have some effect on what you do. The inaccurate results of a simple blood test to look for HIV antibodies can have immediate and devastating consequences for the life of an individual. The married, pregnant woman who is falsely diagnosed as HIV-positive, for example, might begin a series of cascading events that will likely start with questions about her husband and his fidelity.

On the other hand, a false negative in any kind of diagnostic test can be very dangerous when it results in an undiagnosed medical problem's going unattended and unresolved. Most normal ranges for test results are derived statistically from results in normal individuals. Occasionally, however, 'normal' for one person will fall outside this statistical norm. What this means for you is that even a seemingly abnormal finding might actually be normal for you.

Safety is another issue when it comes to testing. Most of us recognize that there are certain risks involved in the treatment of illnesses. For example, there are small (and usually acceptable) risks in any surgery that requires anaesthetic. There are risks involved in taking any new medication. But few of us realize that there are risks involved even in diagnostic testing.

Consider the young woman who goes to her doctor with pain in the upper right quadrant of her abdomen. The first thing the doctor thinks about is gallstones, so he or she sends the patient off for an ultrasound. The ultrasound shows something on her liver, and this needs further investigation. Because it might be a liver tumour, the patient is sent for a CT scan where she is injected with dye. She has never had this dye before: she has a severe allergic reaction and dies.

We might look at this story in a slightly different way. The patient has the enhanced CT scan, and it clearly shows a tumour. Without actually looking at the tissue, though, the doctors don't know whether the tumour is benign, in which case it requires no treatment, or malignant, in which case it definitely needs to be treated. So it is necessary to get a piece of this tumour. The doctors order a liver biopsy but, because liver tumours are usually made up of many blood vessels and carry a high risk of bleeding when a needle is inserted into them, the doctors do what is called an 'open' biopsy. This entails a general anaesthetic, a surgical incision, and several days in hospital. The specimen taken turns out to be benign, so no treatment is ordered. However, during surgery, the tumour's blood vessels are damaged, they bleed profusely – and the patient dies.

Obviously, a smart patient recognizes that there are risks involved in even seemingly simple diagnostic procedures. You should ensure that your questions are answered before agreeing to any tests. Keep in mind too that one test can lead to another, as in the above example. You may think that you are submitting to a simple blood test, but, because some results can point vaguely in one direction or another, further testing is often needed. This can lead to more and more invasive procedures.

Why so many?

It's as if you've gotten on some kind of a merry-go-round, and you can't get off. That's the feeling you get when you begin a series of diagnostic tests. One seems to lead to another, with no end in sight. If the doctors look long enough, they're bound to find something. Why do doctors and especially hospitals seem to order so many tests on people? There are several reasons.

First, and perhaps most annoying, is that some tests are 'routine.' When you are admitted to a hospital, there are likely to be specific tests to which every patient is submitted, regardless of complaint. For example, a series of blood screening tests is the norm in a lot of places. Also, for many years, all patients admitted to hospitals were required to have chest X-rays. This was a throw-back to the days of tuberculosis. Most hospitals today recognize that the risks of overexposure to X-rays, not to mention the outrageous costs, outweigh any benefits gained from such wide-scale screening. Now, only those patients whose medical history indicates a reason will have a chest X-ray. In addition, blood testing for syphilis used to be routine; patients rarely knew that one of the blood samples they supplied was for this.

Then, there are those tests that are routinely ordered for patients admitted to specific units. If you are admitted to the cardiac floor, your doctor will have routine tests for heart disease. If you are admitted for surgery, you may find yourself subjected to routine pre-operative testing, which can involve blood tests, urine tests, and, sometimes, X-rays. Table 8.1 lists some of the typical 'routine' tests done on patients when admitted to hospital.

The second reason that the physician seems to reach for the test requisition pad more frequently today than ever before is for self-protection. With fear of being sued increasingly on their minds, many doctors want to ensure that they cannot be accused of neglecting to look down any path for a potential cause of a medical complaint. This fear can lead to overtesting.

The third reason, which is of more concern in the United States than in Canada, is that diagnostic testing can be very lucrative. If a group of doctors owns a particular piece of diagnostic equipment, for example, such as a mammography machine, they have to pay for it. Using it is the easiest way to recoup the expense. More than anything else, the privatization of diagnostic services is likely to be the explanation for overtesting. We'll look more at system overuse in chapter 15.

Another reason for so many tests, and one that you won't like, is that patients often demand them. A young woman who complains of severe headaches, for example, demands that she needs a CT scan, when her symptoms clearly demonstrate that her headaches are stress-related. The physician may order the scan, and when the results indicate nothing wrong, the patient demands to have the test repeated.

Yet another reason so many tests are sometimes ordered is the seductive lure of new technology. Some doctors simply seem to

Table 8.1
Sample 'Routine' Tests

If you ...	You will likely require the following 'routine' tests when admitted to a hospital ...
are over 60	electrocardiogram (ECG), complete blood count (CBC, includes counting red and white cells and hemoglobin)
are currently pregnant	CBC
have heavy or frequent periods	CBC
are possibly pregnant	pregnancy test
have heart trouble, angina, or palpitations	ECG
have had heart attack, heart murmur, or rheumatic fever	ECG, CBC, chest X-ray, creatinine (blood test)
have lung disease	CBC, ECG, chest X-ray
have cancer	CBC, ECG, chest X-ray, liver enzymes
have diabetes	CBC, ECG, creatinine, blood sugar
have liver disease	CBC, blood tests for liver enzymes and bleeding factors
have kidney disease or urinary tract problems	CBC creatinine, electrolytes (blood test)
are on dialysis	ECG, CBC, creatinine, electrolytes
are taking water pills	ECG, creatinine, electrolytes
are taking digitalis preparations	ECG, creatinine, electrolytes, serum digoxin
are taking steroids	electrolytes, blood sugar
are taking blood thinners (or if you bruise easily)	CBC and blood test for bleeding factors

get a heady feeling from the knowledge that their hospital or clinic has just acquired a new technological marvel. If it's there, why not use it? Well, because you may not need it. Perhaps you need to discuss with the doctor what she or he would have done last month before that new equipment arrived.

Can you refuse to have a test? Certainly. If the nurse who says you have to have a chest X-ray when you've been admitted to have your bunions surgically removed can't provide you with a satisfactory explanation of why it needs to be done, you can simply refuse to have it. This will likely result in a good explanation forthcoming from someone else, or you will have saved yourself from an unnecessary test and the system from using resources unnecessarily.

Commonly ordered tests

If you were to follow a group of doctors on rounds in a hospital or observe a family doctor during an average office day, you would find that there are certain tests that are commonly ordered. In fact, you or someone in your family has probably had every one of them in recent years.

Most people are aware that doctors take samples of urine and blood on a regular basis. The tests they order to be done on these samples supply them with a variety of useful information. We provide you with some very basic information in table 8.2 to enable you to begin to understand what the laboratory technologists, X-ray technicians, and others do with these requisitions from doctors.

This is not an exhaustive discussion of common tests. We developed this list from experience in hospitals and doctors' offices so that you can begin to think about the kinds of questions you might ask.

Not-so-commonly ordered tests

Then there are the not-so-common tests. There are several reasons why they are less commonly ordered than the ones we have already discussed.

First, the commonly ordered tests are often ones that can provide a doctor with a wide variety of general information about your health. The results provide a starting point for diagnosis, allowing the doctor to zero in on more specific areas, if necessary.

Table 8.2
Common Diagnostic Tests

Test	involves ...	can find out ...
biopsies	removal of an actual piece of tissue (e.g., a mole) for the cells be examined under a microscope	what the specimen is made up of, especially determining if cancerous cells are present
CBC (complete blood count)	blood sample for lab analysis of blood components	normalcy of blood cells (can indicate infectious processes, anemia, leukemia, etc.)
cultures	swabs or specimens of bodily fluids to be examined for micro-organisms	if there is an infectious process going on and what organism is causing it
ECG, EKG (electro-cardiogram)	placing electrodes on the chest wall to obtain a tracing of the heart's electrical conduction system	if the electrical conduction is normal (damage may cause it to be abnormal), where damage may be located
SMAC	blood sample for lab analysis of blood chemistry	how a number of systems or organs are functioning (e.g., liver)
ultrasound (sonogram)	bouncing sound waves off internal structures to see them (generally painless)	whether the overall structure is normal (e.g., during pregnancy)
urinalysis	providing a urine sample for laboratory testing of chemical composition; may detect micro-organisms	primarily how kidneys are functioning
X-ray (radiograph)	using radiation to take a flat picture of the solid structures inside the body (a mammogram is a breast X-ray)	if structures are abnormal, if fractures are present

Second, the commonly ordered tests are widely available. The corollary of this is that the less commonly ordered tests are often available only in specialized areas. A CT scan, for example, might provide useful information, but it is usually available only in larger centres. This means that the patient may have to travel to have it. The doctor might use a variety of other more easily accessible routes first.

This leads us to the third reason for the less common use of some tests. Often requiring high tech, sophisticated equipment and/or specialized personnel, many of them are expensive. If a more common, less expensive test will provide the needed information, then the more expensive one may not be necessary. This leaves the equipment and expertise required to perform these less common tests available for those patients who truly need them. Table 8.3 provides some information for you on some less commonly used tests that you may need to know about. Keep in mind that our definition of 'less common' is related to the overall use of tests. Clearly, an echocardiogram, for example, is certainly not uncommon in the practice of a cardiologist (a specialist in heart disease), nor is a bone marrow aspiration test in that of a haematologist (a specialist in diseases of the blood).

Tests are not everything

The smart patient needs to know something about the relationship between the advancing role of biotechnology and the use of diagnostic testing in the practice of medicine.

In the early years of the twentieth century, doctors really had little more than their own senses to make observations about the patient. Diagnosis was an art, and its scientific aspects had yet to be discovered. Thus, the skills of the individual doctor were key. The practice of medicine, however, has changed.

Research and development in the biotechnology industries have provided physicians with great assistance in the art, and now science, of diagnosis. The down side to this is that, today, diseases are often not given enough time to declare themselves, so to speak. In the mad dash toward the 'quick fix,' the doctor, often aided and abetted by the impatient patient, rushes the patient onto the merry-go-round of medical diagnosis. Another important set of collaborators in this mad dash are the companies that

Table 8.3
Less Common Diagnostic Tests

Test	involves ...	can show ...
arteriogram	dye injected into arteries in various areas	how blood is flowing; existence of structural abnormalities
bone marrow aspiration	needle inserted into a bone in hip (used to be breastbone)	if your bone marrow is producing normal blood cells
CT (computerized tomography) scans	X-ray (sometimes enhanced by injection of dye into blood stream)	3D pictures of the inside of your body
Doppler flow studies	ultrasound	blood flow in various parts of your body
echocardiogram	ultrasound of the heart	structure of the heart
IVP (intravenous pyelogram)	dye injected into a vein and X-ray	picture of blood flow in the kidneys
lumbar puncture	removal of small amount of spinal fluid via a needle into spine	abnormalities of fluid or injuries
MRI (magnetic resonance imaging)	uses a magnet and radio waves bounced off body structures	detailed imaging pictures of various layers of internal structures
-scopes	insertion of a small, lighted instrument into the body	real views of internal structures (or surgery can be performed this way)

develop and manufacture the new technological marvels. If you ran a company that produces CT scanners, wouldn't your bottom line be influenced by the number of doctors who order such tests? It's worth thinking about.

9

Drugs – Keeping the Lid On

Doctors are men who prescribe medicine of which they know little to cure diseases of which they know less in human beings of which they know nothing.

Voltaire (1694–1778)

Pete's rotation on orthopaedic surgery under the tutelage of Dr Backman had come to an end, and he had mixed feelings about it. He had really liked the idea of bone surgery and had considered pursuing a specialty in that area, but Dr Backman's personality had put him off. Pete, however, still had another year of his two-year internship, so he had several months yet before he had to apply for his residency. Or, he could open a general practice. There would be so many decisions to make. Some could wait.

Today, he began his eight weeks on general medicine. On this rotation, Pete would see a little bit of everything. He hoped that his knowledge of drugs and therapeutics would improve, because he felt distinctly uncomfortable with what he knew about medications. He had attended numerous lectures in medical school, but medication preparations seemed to change so often and so many were similar. The pharmaceutical companies appeared to be coming out with so-called new and improved drugs every month. Pete sighed and patted the pharmacology handbook he had tucked into his already bulging lab coat pockets.

He was on his way to do an admission examination on Mrs Fielding, a 65-year-old patient who had just been admitted after having what was believed to be a mild stroke. As he arrived at the door of her room, he looked down to check the number to make sure it was correct. In that split second that his head was down, a nurse burst out of the door carrying a large brown paper bag. The collision was spectacular. As they crashed into one another, the bag burst and little bottles spilled out. Because some of the lids were not on tightly, pills spilled out onto the linoleum floor, rolling along like so many tiny marbles.

'Oh, my – ' the nurse gasped as she realized what had happened. She and Pete stood up and looked at each other and then at the floor.

'Welcome to General Medicine, Dr Kowalski. I'm Kate Johnson, the team leader, and these,' she said with a gesture toward the floor, 'are Mrs Fielding's medications. Any questions?'

Pete considered all the colours, sizes, and shapes of the pills that lay about their feet. There were tiny white ones, medium pink ones, large two-coloured ones. There were round ones, oval ones, and even one or two square ones. *What* they all were was quite another question to be answered. Pete and Kate looked at each other and started laughing.

He bent down and began examining the pill bottles. 'Well,' he said, 'I did want to learn more about drugs. There's nothing like starting at the bottom and working up. I guess I now know how many medications Mrs Fielding's been on.' He looked up at Kate as he examined the tiniest pill he had ever seen. 'I think you better call me Pete.'

They started cleaning up the mess they had made.

SO, YOU THINK PETE'S EXPERIENCE IS LUDICROUS? You think maybe it's too far from the truth to make a good point? Better start thinking again.

It is widely known among members of the medical profession that older people and people in hospitals are likely to be on more medications than the average younger, non-hospitalized person. When it comes to drugs, however, how much is too much for you?

As far as medications are concerned, being a smart patient requires two things. First, you need to develop an attitude that drugs are servants, not masters. Second, you need to understand what influences both your and your doctor's choices when it comes to choosing whether to use drugs and which ones.

Selling drugs to docs

You've seen the commercials in recent years. He talks about his 'motility' problem, and his stomach begins blowing up. She wears a hat and begins to talk about not believing it could ever happen to her (hair loss, that is). You never hear the actual name of a drug, and you might even have a tough time figuring out that this commercial is, in fact, about a specific drug. Then they give you an '800' number to call for information and indicate the name of the (pharmaceutical) company sponsoring the advertisement. You may be inclined to think that they are just going to give you information about the illness in question. Make no mistake, the ad is for a prescription drug. The advertiser wants you to go to your doctor and ask for that specific prescription drug for your health problem.

What's wrong with this picture? On the face of it, probably nothing. The issue here, however, is that this is just another avenue to sell drugs to doctors. The only difference is now *you* are the one doing the selling for the company, and you're not even getting a commission.

Drug companies sell drugs to doctors in a variety of ways. The first and probably classic way that doctors are introduced to new preparations (as well as old ones) is through a sales pitch by what used to be known as the drug 'detail man.' The modern pharmaceutical sales representative (who is more likely to be a woman) does the same thing. He or she visits doctors in a specific sales territory on a regular basis to provide oral and written information, and less and less frequently now, samples.

Drug companies also use direct mail to sell to doctors. Using talented marketing and advertising teams, the companies design elaborate brochures to catch the physician's attention. These expensive marketing tools are often casually tossed into the wastebasket without the doctor even glancing at them.

Direct selling to physicians, however, is becoming part of medical history. Pharmaceutical companies are more likely to spend their time, money, and other resources on influencing the people who decide which drugs go on the 'approved' (in other words, approved for payment) drug list developed by health maintenance organizations (HMO)'s in the United States and by provincial pharmacare programs in Canada.

These are the direct and easily identifiable ways that drugs are sold to doctors. Some of the other tactics are more subtle.

The soft sell

For any other kind of company that sells a consumable product, it is simply 'business as usual' to advertise their wares to the people most likely to influence the consumption of the product. This is what pharmaceutical companies do, but they also use some less overt marketing tactics. In fact, in recent years, these companies have become expert at finding new and improved ways of influencing the prescribing habits of our doctors. As you have already seen, even you, the patient, are now being used as a marketing vehicle.

One awe-inspiring approach that drug companies regularly use is to support continuing medical education programs for doctors. This has become a tradition, almost an institution. If you look at the printed program for a continuing education conference for doctors, you will see a list of sponsors prominently displayed. What's amazing is the number of such events and the perks that go along with each one (such as cocktails, followed by a presentation, followed by a lavish dinner).

With increased attention being paid to the ethical aspects of the relationship between physicians and pharmaceutical companies with regard to influence in prescribing, guidelines for such financial support have become more rigorous. Medical schools, which rely heavily on such support to provide continuing education to practising physicians, are increasingly careful to keep the companies at arm's length. Still, there are many opportunities for doctors to partake in lectures-cum-dinner where the speaker and the meal are paid for by the pharmaceutical company and where use of that company's drug will be prominent in the cases discussed. A recent mini-survey on our part found that more than a dozen invitations to such events made their way into our office in a two-month period. This is in one small Canadian city.

Drug companies continue to advertise their products in publications designed specifically for doctors. In fact, many of these publications would not exist without the advertising revenues provided by pharmaceutical manufacturers. Other forms of promotion to doctors are in the form of what physicians refer to as 'throw-away journals.' In one six-month period, over fifty such unrequested periodicals found their way into our office.

Typically, such publications contain articles ostensibly written by medical experts about specific topics. Often, however, these articles are the work of medical writers who compile information provided by the physicians who agree to have their names attached to them. For example, a medical writer might attend a lecture given by a consultant and then write an article for a publication. Many such articles have a slant toward the use of drugs manufactured by the organization sponsoring the lecture or relate only the results of studies favouring the use of these drugs. Unlike articles published in reputable medical journals, these papers are not 'peer-reviewed.'

Drug companies used to provide medical students, interns, residents, and practising physicians alike with a variety of paraphernalia emblazoned with corporate names and logos. Pocket protectors, pens, note pads, prescription pads(!), coffee mugs, computers, and briefcases were often in evidence in hospitals and offices, and ball caps, tee-shirts, athletic bags, and even golf tees with these corporate logos could be found enhancing the doctor's image when off-duty. Pharmaceutical companies have even supplied newly graduating physicians with their 'black bags.' This approach to marketing has gone out of favour with the companies as professional medical associations have begun

to caution their members about the potential influence of accepting such 'freebies.'

Researchers at Case Western Reserve University in Cleveland
wanted to know whether interaction with specific drug company
representatives had any effect on physicians' prescribing
behaviour. They found that doctors who had recently met with
specific drug company representatives were about four times more
likely to request brand-name drugs than doctors in a control group
who had not had such interactions. Perhaps more startling was
the finding that these doctors requesting brand-name drugs were
two and a half times more likely to have accepted funds from
that drug company to attend a meeting, give a presentation, or
undertake research (Gullens 1992).

Drugs as servant, not master

Progress in the use of pharmaceutical preparations to aid in the
treatment and even cure of diseases represents a major advance
of medicine in the twentieth century. Some of the discoveries
were made serendipitously by researchers while looking for something else. Penicillin is a prime example of this process; it was not
developed after years of painstaking research and development
by a drug company. Nevertheless, the drug companies and their
wares do, indeed, have a place in your health care. You just have
to be smart about how you and your doctor together make decisions about what that place is.

Sometimes, drugs are used for convenience. It's easier to take
a medication to treat a symptom than it is to take alternative
action. For example, a doctor may prescribe a drug for you to
ease the pain of your arthritis. On the face of it, this seems rea-
sonable. If, however, you are eighty pounds overweight, the stress
on your joints may be causing you more pain than you might
have if you were to lose weight. Losing weight, though, is often
no easy feat. But if your doctor sends you to a nutritionist, puts
you on an exercise program, and follows up on this, you may
find a decreased need for the medication. Between you and your
doctor, you need to explore the options for treatment. The alternative to the little pill may be more difficult, but do keep in mind

that there isn't a drug preparation around that is without side effects.

Make sure that you aren't the one who is encouraging your doctor to reach for that prescription pad. Doctors often hear the lament, 'Can't you just give me a pill for it, doc?' A smart patient will use his or her time with the doctor to explore the alternatives to 'the little pill.'

Drugs are treatment modalities that need to be fully understood by the patient. Recently, pharmacists have expanded their role to include more patient counselling about drug regimens. They even have access to a variety of computerized drug education programs. Your filled prescription today is likely to come to you accompanied by extensive literature for your education. As a patient, this probably seems like a good thing. To your doctor, however, it may not be as welcome. (See our discussion of questions to ask your pharmacist in chapter 5.) There is a growing undercurrent of concern among many physicians about this expanding role for pharmacists. Although doctors rarely voice their objections to the concept, what they do about it is another story.

Doctors base their opposition on a well-known fact about human beings: we are very suggestible. So, even though it may appear comforting and perhaps even safe to know all manner of potential side effects to the drugs you're taking, it is probably more useful to know and truly understand the most important of those possible side effects. If you are told that a newly prescribed medication may cause nausea, there is a greater chance that you will experience nausea. (This is one potential side effect listed for almost every medication on the market, as someone somewhere attributed nausea to the drug at some point in its history.) This can be important to your health. If a medication that is otherwise effective must be discontinued by you because of the information you received, this service does you a disservice.

If you know yourself well enough to realize that you tend to be nervous about new medications or you are hypochondriacal, ask the pharmacist to give you a list of only the most serious potential side effects. This will require the pharmacist to talk to you, rather than to simply pull something off the computer. This personal interaction is likely to be a much higher quality health service than a computer program spewing out the same information for every person.

The bottom line on drugs

The use of pharmaceutical preparations is a big part of health care. As we've already said, this is perhaps one of the most important advances in health care in this century. It may also be one of the biggest problems. The bottom line is that drugs are here to stay. The smart patient will be aware of this and know how to handle his or her doctor when it comes to that prescription pad.

If medications are a regular part of your own health care, ask your doctor from time to time if one or more of them might be discontinued. Changes in your health status may allow this to occur.

Always take the lowest effective dose of any medication. Discuss this with your doctor and avoid self-medication. If you are on a prescription drug, and it seems to be effective, don't ever assume that more of the same will be better. It is more likely to have a negative effect on you.

Be aware of addicting medications. Drug dependence is not just an issue for the street-dwelling junkie. There are several classes of drugs, including things such as sleeping pills, pain medications, and diet pills, that can be addictive. Discuss these carefully with your doctor and take them only as long as they are required by the state of your health.

As a smart patient, you are in control of your drug consumption.

10
High Tech Reality

Science is a first-rate piece of furniture for a man's upper chamber, if
he has common sense on the ground floor.

Oliver Wendell Holmes (1872)

Pete was excited about his new rotation. Two gruelling months
dealing with mostly chronic, debilitated patients whose potential
for recovery was questionable at best, were finally over. Pete was
leaving the medical school affiliated hospital, where there were
wall-to-wall interns, residents, and medical school faculty, to
spend a month at what was euphemistically referred to as 'Elsewhere General.' This was not to be mistaken for the hospital in
the old television program 'St Elsewhere.' Long before the pro-
ducers of that show put the phrase in their title, medical school
faculty and students used it to refer (and not necessarily in a
complimentary way) to hospitals outside of their realm. Pete was
going to a community hospital to get a taste of intensive care
medicine at the front line of the war against illness.

Pete expected this rotation to be interesting and more relaxing
than an intensive care rotation in a large, teaching hospital. He
was wrong. He found that out his first night on-call.

It was 4:15 a.m. when the charge nurse in the ICU started bang-
ing on the door to the duty room.

'Dr Kowalski, you better get up,' she said as loudly as she
could, given that the room was opposite the first patient cubicle.

Pete pulled his white lab coat on over the ever-present operating room greens he slept in and headed toward the nursing station. Pandemonium. There had been an accident, and Pete was receiving two admissions, one to be prepped for abdominal surgery to stop internal bleeding. The other was a 17-year-old boy who had been thrown off his motorcycle when it hit a van. On the outside, the boy didn't look bad, with just some bruises and a broken leg, but what was going on inside his head was of disaster proportions.

The ambulance attendants had started an IV in the boy's left arm, and one of the nurses was efficiently placing electrodes on his chest and hooking him up to a heart monitor. He had a catheter into his bladder to drain urine, and an air splint on his left leg. The respiratory technologist was using an Ambu bag to inflate his lungs, while the other nurse prepared the artificial ventilator. The boy wasn't breathing on his own. Worst of all, when Pete shone a light into his eyes, the pupils, which should have constricted in response, remained fixed and dilated. He also was displaying no reflexes. These were ominous signs, indeed.

According to the ambulance attendants' report, the young man had stopped breathing during the ambulance ride, and his pupils had become fixed around the same time.

Pete knew what these signs meant. The patient was probably brain dead. The nurses in the emergency department had telephoned the one neurologist in the town, and he was now on his way to the hospital. Although this certainly wasn't an organ transplant facility, Pete began to wonder if they harvested organs for use in his medical school affiliated hospital, where they had a thriving transplant program.

Once the neurologist arrived, events unfolded quickly. Brain death was diagnosed, and the neurologist approached the parents for consent to remove their son's organs for transplant. Pete notified the transplant coordinator at the university hospital, who had already put the preliminary wheels in motion but was awaiting the family's final response to the donation request. Overwhelmed by grief and disbelief, the parents didn't know what to do. They wanted more time to decide and to take in all that had just happened. Unfortunately, there wasn't much time. The young man's blood pressure was unstable, as happens in such cases, and, although the nurses and doctors were doing all they could, the boy's organs would only be usable if removed while they were still getting a good blood supply.

It was as unpleasant a situation as Pete had ever found himself in. He was providing skilled medical care for a dead person. The patient was dead, but his heart was beating. No wonder the family was having such a hard time. Pete knew that advances in high technology medicine had brought him to this.

High technology medicine can be likened to a monster which, feeding on brilliant discoveries, medical egos, media attention and the free enterprise system, has grown to such unwieldy proportions that it threatens to engulf us if we do not learn to use it more wisely. (Parsons and Parsons 1992, 75)

HIGH TECHNOLOGY MEDICINE is exciting, and it has contributed in no small way to improved quality of life for many people. Its overuse, misuse, and the average person's misunderstanding of what it entails, however, are problems for the smart patient.

The dilemma in which both Pete and the unfortunate patient's family found themselves is an invention of the late twentieth century. Apart from the actual technology itself, this is the stuff of the front-page news, the headlines, the high profile stories, and the people. So often it involves dramatic events and situations and plays to the North American desire for the 'quick fix' for what ails us. These technological marvels, however, do not always result in the fast and dramatic results so frequently portrayed in the popular media. Let's go behind the doors of an intensive care unit in a large teaching hospital to see and hear things that you might otherwise not be privy to.

Life in the ICU

Our tour begins outside the entrance to the intensive care unit. This is where the most seriously ill patients in the entire hospital are housed. The receptionist outside the imposing, visually impenetrable doors is officious and needs to know exactly who you are, whom you wish to see, and what your business is. He or she tells you exactly how long you may stay behind the doors. You feel like saluting before you enter the mysterious halls. But if you actually have a family member inside, you are probably distraught, and his or her manner is just an impediment to your progress.

Once inside the ICU, you observe a controlled frenzy of activity. There are rhythmic, swishing sounds, faint beeping at various pitches, muffled voices. You have probably only heard these noises on television medical dramas. And so much to see!

First, we observe the people who work here. The nurses seem young. They don't appear to be new graduates, but they hardly look ready for retirement. Perhaps ICU is a specialty for the younger breed. The nurses seem efficient and calm, despite the desperate sickness of the people in the beds and the vast array of equipment, so frightening to the uninitiated.

Suddenly, the calm is shattered. A patient's heart has stopped beating, and the staff members leap into action. Each one knows his or her role well. There is no room for error or confusion in this situation.

More machinery arrives, as if by magic, and it is used efficiently and sometimes effectively.

But in this case, the patient is an older man with significant heart disease, and this is not the first time he has suffered a cardiac arrest. He had never regained consciousness after the last resuscitation, and this time the medical team is unable to 'bring him back.' The patient is dead.

But wait a minute. Before we move on, you notice something odd happening. A medical student is taking an instrument called a laryngoscope off the tray on the overbed table. A laryngoscope has a curved blade with a light, and it is used to pass into a patient's throat to guide a breathing (endotracheal) tube into the trachea to connect the patient to an artificial ventilator. Why is she doing this after the patient has been declared dead? You listen for a minute. The medical student is practising. Hmm.

Modern reverence for high tech

How are high tech approaches to health care delivery viewed within the medical care system? Without a doubt hospitals today are different places than they were even thirty years ago. Technology has been playing an ever increasing role in both the diagnosis (as we mentioned in chapter 8 when discussing tests) and the treatment of disease. It is, however, important to note that not all medical specialties rely equally on technology. Family physicians, pediatricians, and psychiatrists, for example, are at the low tech end of medical practice. What's even more telling, though, is that these are the areas that are on the lowest end of the fee scale. In other words, from a financial point of view, modern North American society values the more technologically oriented approaches to medical care more highly and places less value on medicine, the art.

The same trend can be seen in the field of nursing. Many current nursing contracts provide for a premium on the salary of nurses who choose to work in such areas as intensive care, coronary care, post-operative recovery rooms, operating rooms, and other technologically oriented areas. Historically, it was deemed that these nurses would require specialized training and, thus, were entitled to higher compensation. It is difficult, however, to place relative value on skills. Who possesses the more valuable skills – the nurse who will work a twelve-hour night shift caring for one critically ill patient, in an intensive care unit surrounded by a maze of equipment, or the nurse who works the night in charge of an oncology unit where forty patients are suffering from cancer, and where she (or he) may spend part of the night supporting a family and holding the hand of a patient as he slips toward a quiet death – with no lights flashing and no bells ringing?

As a health care consumer, you are to some extent also responsible for this evident reverence for all that is high tech. With media stories playing up the glamour of new and exciting procedures, you as a consumer may be among those who demand more and more in the way of high technology approaches. All of us need to be more critical media consumers, and we all need to seek further information, for the media rarely tell us the entire story.

Fall-out of high tech

Technological advances have had major effects on health care, in the general sense, but also in the individual doctor–patient encounter. First, broadly, you may have already wondered which health care professional has the expertise to use some of these new technological marvels as they are developed. One outcome of all this has been the proliferation of new allied health professionals. It's become difficult enough to know who's who in health care, because with almost every advance in technology comes a new kind of health professional.

- Open heart surgery and the heart–lung machine require perfusionists to operate the machinery.
- Advances in bone and skin transplantation require tissue bank technicians.
- Ultrasound technology requires ultrasound technicians.
- The growth in the high tech equipment industry in general has led to the need for biomedical engineers.

The second broad outcome of technological advance has been the evolution of the 'fix-it' mentality among both members of the medical profession and average North American consumers of health care. Think about your own attitude. When you enter your doctor's office, do you go in with the attitude of 'just fix it, doc'? A smart patient won't adopt this attitude; nor will a smart patient expect the doctor to have it.

High tech advances have, indeed, had an effect on how you, the patient, are treated both by your doctor and by the system in general. First, in many ways, high technology places a barrier between the doctor and the patient. Sometimes it is an actual physical barrier. A patient in the intensive care unit who is on a heart monitor, for example, can be partially examined from the nursing station, as the nurses and doctors study the remote display of the cardiac monitor. Or, the doctor who relies heavily on technological approaches to diagnosis may not often enough use and therefore maintain the clinical skills of observation, auscultation, and intuition in top-notch form.

More often, however, the barrier is psychological. As a patient, you can begin to feel that you have a better relationship with a piece of equipment than with your doctor, for you probably have spent more time with that piece of equipment. Thus, technology has made its insidious way into that most intimate relationship – the one between you and your doctor.

The second personal effect of too much use of high tech equipment in medicine is the tendency for some physicians to begin to lose sight of their patients as whole human beings, and see them more as the sum of their parts – chemicals, organs, and systems. A doctor can break you down into such small fragments that he or she may tend to think about you more as your potassium level, for example, because that's what he or she is treating.

This fragmentation of the individual patient, much bemoaned by adherents of the less mainstream approaches to medicine, can result in a dehumanization of the entire process. Sickness loses its meaning as a personal human experience. As difficult as illness is, there is little doubt that many people actually grow through the process. Seeing the illness as part of yourself can help you cope with its outcomes, especially when, because of the nature of your illness, modern medicine isn't offering you much help.

Finally, and perhaps most crucially to the smart patient, is that reliance on high technology in diagnosis and therapeutics can make you feel as if you have totally lost control of your own health care. Now it's in the hands of technicians and their machinery. This is because the results of one technological procedure can lead easily to another, and another. The smart patient needs to avoid this loss of control.

If you are having difficulty making sense of the morass of information and choices facing you, you may need to involve an advocate. Get a trusted family member to run interference for you while you try to sort out what you want and what you don't. Make sure you stay in control. You want a doctor who sees you as a whole person with both a body and a spirit. Such doctors *are* out there!

11

Operation Necessary?

Now it cannot be too often repeated that when an operation is once performed, nobody can ever prove that it was unnecessary ... Operation is therefore the safe side for the surgeon as well as the lucrative side.

George Bernard Shaw (1856–1950)
The Doctor's Dilemma

Eleanor Gass needed to have her gallbladder removed. When her doctor broke the news, she had just recently found a routine again, with her father settled in a long-term care facility to recover from his surgery. She didn't really welcome yet another upheaval in her life, but the pain in the right upper quadrant of her abdomen wasn't pleasant to live with either. So she agreed to see the surgeon.

Dr Antonia Grimaldi was young for a surgeon, or so Eleanor thought. She looked to Eleanor more like the model for a cosmetic company. Should she trust her gallbladder to this woman? When Dr Grimaldi started examining her and talking to her, all of Eleanor's doubts faded away. For all her dark beauty, this woman knew what she was doing.

Eleanor now felt that she was in good hands as she waited on her stretcher in the corridor outside the operating room. With the medication from her pre-operative needle moving through her veins, she was feeling happily languid, when young Dr Pete Kowalski stopped by and lifted her chart from its place by her feet.

Just back from Elsewhere General, Pete had begun his surgical rotation this very morning, and Dr Grimaldi was the surgeon to whose service he was assigned.

'Hello, Mrs Gass,' he said smiling, 'nice to see you again. I notice that you're the patient this time.'

'Yes, Dr Kowalski,' said Eleanor. 'I guess you're going to help Dr Grimaldi take out this darned gallbladder.'

Pete examined both Eleanor and her chart briefly and told her that the anaesthetist would be by shortly and that they would be taking her inside in about ten minutes.

'How's your father?' he asked before he left.

'Coming along well. He doesn't love it at the facility where he is, but he's looking forward to getting well enough to go home. He's so stubborn, you know.'

Pete laughed. His assessment of Mr Frail was that he was so independent-minded that a daughter might perceive that to be stubbornness. He headed toward the scrub sinks where the resident was already hard at work washing his forearms.

A few minutes later, a nurse came and wheeled Eleanor into the operating room. Eleanor felt a slight chill. 'Everything is so clean and cold-looking,' she thought. She was trying desperately to take it all in so that she might allay some of her fears of being put under an anaesthetic.

Before long, however, the anaesthetic had taken effect, and Eleanor was oblivious to her surroundings. The nurse began to prep her skin. She peeled off the 'johnny shirt,' and, using a long-handled forceps and series of cotton swabs, she began to paint an orangey substance over Eleanor's abdomen. After each swirl, the nurse threw the swab into a bucket on the floor and took a fresh one. Pete and the resident walked in the door.

'Another fat, female, and forty,' Joe, the resident, said snidely, looking at Eleanor's exposed, now yellow abdomen.

Pete winced. He knew that Eleanor couldn't hear them, but still, he always wondered. The resident had repeated an old and long-discarded saying doctors had for patients who needed to have their gallbladders out; it had never been meant in a very complimentary way. Pete also knew that as nice as Joe was, his major flaw was an inability to keep his sexist remarks to himself. Pete had heard stories of his fiery encounters with Dr Grimaldi.

Joe made another couple of comments about female anatomy, and then Dr Grimaldi backed into the room, her freshly scrubbed hands held high in the air.

'I trust we're going to have a pleasant morning, Dr Smith,' she said to Joe. 'Just keep your tongue still, and maybe our new intern will get a favourable impression of us.'

She nodded to the circulating nurse who came over to tie Dr Grimaldi's surgical gown and help her on with her sterile gloves. The circulating nurse was not scrubbed so that she could 'circulate' in and out of the operating theatre to retrieve things that might be needed and touch non-sterile pieces of equipment and supplies.

The scrub nurse, gowned, masked, and gloved, was already laying out the sterile instruments. She would assist the doctors. The circulating nurse turned on the stereo and Dr Grimaldi asked for a scalpel.

Loud strains of Vivaldi effectively drowned out conversation. Pete found it hard to concentrate with noise; he always had. Dr Grimaldi, however, thrived on the loud classical music, and today, this was her operating room. Pete hoped he wouldn't lose his grip on the retractor he was holding.

As with many medical students, Pete had always disliked the sight of blood. During the first operation he had ever seen, he had felt so woozy he had had to leave. At least he hadn't fainted! The head nurse had issued an instruction, saying that if you were going to faint, to fall backward, and not onto the operating table. The students had all laughed derisively – and then two of them actually fainted.

Pete was more used to it now, but he still marvelled at the popularity of the television show *Operation*, not to mention some of the even more popular prime time medical dramas like *ER* that made ample use of film footage of actual blood and guts. Who could ever predict what would capture the public's interest?

And then, his worst fears came true. He dropped a heavy retractor on Eleanor's leg. Joe looked over and laughed.

'The old girl's going to wonder where she got the bruise on her leg when she wakes up. Don't worry, Kowalski. It happens all the time. Patients just wake up with bruises in the oddest places. Last Tuesday ...'

Joe trailed off as Dr Grimaldi glared at him.

'Get me another one, Dr Kowalski,' she said.

When you're holding a hammer ...

There's an old saying: 'When you're holding a hammer, everything looks like a nail.' There's a related saying that's common in medical circles: 'When in doubt, cut it out.'

If you've ever been faced with the news that you need an operation, you probably didn't look forward to it with the same anticipation you might associate with going on a long-awaited vacation. Indeed, most of us dread 'going under the knife.' But we know that advances in surgical techniques over the past few decades have saved innumerable lives and improved the lives of countless others. Surgical approaches to fixing what's wrong with you are certainly beneficial aspects of modern medicine. Still, smart patients will have questions:

• How is this operation likely to benefit me?
• What risks does the operation pose?
• What is likely to happen to me and my health without this operation?
• Are there any alternative, less invasive treatment approaches for this problem?
• How do the risks and benefits of the alternatives compare with those of the operation?
• If I conclude that the operation is necessary, how can I be a smart patient?

Whether a particular surgical procedure is necessary is a question asked ever more frequently among health care critics. Recently, the value of some procedures, such as tonsillectomies (removal of the tonsils), cesarean sections, cholecystectomies (gallbladder removals), mastectomies (complete removal of the breast to treat cancer), and hysterectomies (removal of the uterus to treat a variety of conditions) has been questioned. It's not that the critics deem these procedures to be unnecessary in every case. They do believe, however, that more of these procedures are being performed than is medically necessary. For there is some truth in Shaw's literary comment, quoted at the beginning of this chapter. Once a surgical procedure is completed, it can be difficult, indeed, to say what would have happened to that particular patient had the procedure not been done. Surgeons perform surgery. If you are referred to a surgeon, he or she is likely to recommend surgery.

One of the factors that has allegedly had an impact on the dramatic increase in the number of times some surgical procedures are performed is the advent of newer, easier, faster, and safer ways to carry them out. The extent to which this supposition might be true was tested by researchers at the University of Pennsylvania medical school (Escarce, Chen and Schwartz 1995). They examined the histories of almost 54,000 patients who had undergone cholecystectomy between 1986 and 1993. They found that the rates at which this procedure was performed increased 22 per cent between 1989 and 1993. In 1989, surgeons in Pennsylvania had begun using a procedure called a laparoscopic cholecystectomy, where the surgery is done through a scope, rather than through an open incision. Patients recover faster from this procedure, and they spend less time in hospital. Questions remain, however: Did more people actually need the surgery than ever, or did the ease of carrying out the procedure make it simpler to go ahead and do the operation anyway? Did some of the patients opt to have the surgery because the procedure had improved? And, the bottom line question: Were all of these procedures actually medically necessary? Even though, as a patient, you may be in a difficult position to answer these kinds of questions on your own, the important question has to do with *your own* need for surgery. Asking the questions we have suggested and ensuring that you understand the answers you receive will put you in a much better position to answer, at least for yourself.

Blood and guts and fascination

The seductiveness of using new techniques and the higher fees associated with the 'cutting' specialties in medicine probably have some bearing on the attitudes of the medical profession in recommending the use of surgical procedures. The health care consumers also play a part in this upswing.

In the past two or three years we have seen evidence that the general public is becoming more and more fascinated with 'blood and guts.' This fascination is manifested in the popularity of such television shows as the Public Broadcasting System's *Operation*, where the viewer can see real operations in progress, as well as medical dramas such as *Chicago Hope* and *ER*, whose surgical sequences utilize a good dose of footage from real operations. Indeed, even the public fascination with the details of the O.J. Simpson trial in the United States and the Bernardo trial in Canada were examples of a similar interest in gore.

This interest of the general public in surgery can have the result that some patients arrive at their doctors' offices demanding certain types of procedures that they have learned about either on an educational show or on a medical drama. Furthermore, there has been increasing interest among the public in using cosmetic surgery to help them retain a youthful appearance. A smart patient keeps in mind that surgery of any kind doesn't come without risks. There is always the possibility, albeit usually a small one, that something might go wrong. You must understand these risks before you are wheeled into the operating room.

Although for many operations the need is clear-cut, as you can see, increasingly there is evidence that this may not always be the case. Before signing the consent form for any operation, you and your doctor have to explore the risks, benefits, and alternative approaches to treating your problem.

You, under the knife

So you (or a family member) need to have an operation. The prospect isn't at all enticing. You can, however, minimize your psychological discomfort by knowing what is likely to happen to you while you're in hospital and after you return home.

Pre-operative protocols

Before you have an operation, the doctors need to know some things about you. Depending on the type of surgery, the type of information they need can vary, but, in general, the medical people need to know how otherwise healthy you are. Thus, you will have to submit to some blood tests, as well as urine tests and others that may be directly related to the surgery you're having. It used to be that these tests would be performed after your admission to hospital. Today, however, most of them are done prior to your admission, and sometimes even the surgery itself will be done as an out-patient procedure.

Another issue that you need to consider is the need to make an informed decision about your surgery. The notion of patients having the right to 'informed consent' is fairly new. The term was coined in 1957 in the California Court of Appeal (Silverman 1989). The doctor who will perform the surgery (not the nurse or the clerk) must inform you of the risks and benefits of the procedure that he or she will perform. Once you understand this, you can sign the consent form.

Just before

What happens immediately before they wheel you to the operating room can vary with the type of surgery you will be undergoing.

If you are to have a general anaesthetic, you will likely be given a pre-operative medication by injection. This usually consists of something to make you feel drowsy. For you, the effects are twofold: the injection relaxes you during a time when you might be stressed, and it makes it easier for the anaesthetist to put you to sleep.

Hospitals all have their own rules about getting people ready for surgery. You will likely have to lock up your valuables, remove all jewellery and nail polish, and wear a hospital gown.

These rules are not negotiable. The hospital will not take responsibility for your valuables going missing from your bedside table
while you are in the operating room. Your jewellery is considered an unnecessary encumbrance and may get lost or broken (a
necklace, for example) if you do not remove it before you leave
for the OR. Sometimes, hospital personnel will allow you to tape
on a ring that never leaves your finger.

During surgery

You might be stressed out as they wheel you into the operating
room. Remember, however, for the people who work there, this
is an everyday occurrence. Don't be concerned if they seem more
light-hearted than you think they should be. They're not uncon-
cerned about the stress that you feel; they are just more familiar
with what's happening right then than you are.

We're sure you've heard stories about the patient who went in
to have her right leg (or arm or eye) operated on, only to find
afterwards that they had operated on her left one. This does
happen, if only rarely. No matter how insulted they may seem
by your mentioning it, if you are to have one leg, one arm, one
eye, or one ear or whatever operated on, it doesn't hurt to say so
clearly to each person who picks up your chart as you wait.

You're asleep

Once you're asleep, the nurses will position you for the surgery.
Of course, the position depends entirely on what kind of operation you are having. This positioning, however, can often explain
some minor aches and pains that you are likely to experience
after the surgery in areas of your body that seem remote from the
procedure. Ask the surgeon what position you will be in.

Everyone seems to have a small fear of being put under an
anaesthetic and still being able to hear and feel what is going on.
Anecdotal cases of this do appear in medical history, but it is
unlikely to happen. But there does seem to be some evidence that
your subconscious mind is still aware when you are under

anaesthetic and that this part of your consciousness can actually hear. This could mean that negative (or positive) comments made by members of the surgical team while you are asleep might actually have an effect on you. If you've wondered what doctors and nurses really talk about while you're asleep, some of the medical dramas aren't really that far from the truth. Some surgeons expect no chatter whatsoever during the surgery, and others chatter continually themselves. Sometimes the conversation revolves around the procedure itself, especially if there are students observing, in which case the surgeon will actually explain what he or she is doing. But they could also talk about what they did on Saturday night or even tell jokes to one another. These are people at work. They are no different from the rest of us.

You're awake again!

Waking up after surgery is an odd experience. Unlike awaking after a good night's sleep, you feel almost as if a second before you were just nodding off. When you do awake, you will be in the post-anaesthetic recovery room. You will be monitored very closely by the nursing staff, who will take your blood pressure and pulse every five to fifteen minutes, ensuring that you are not slipping into shock. They will check any intravenous equipment that you may have, as well as any dressings. The length of time you spend in this large, bustling room will vary with the type of surgery you have had and, to some extent, with how it went. When you are fully awake enough, you will be discharged from the recovery room and taken back to your own room. Your surgeon may pay you a visit before you are discharged but, except in special circumstances (such as with small children), you will not see any visitors until you return to your room. Many hospitals welcome a parent into the recovery room with a young child, to calm and care for the child.

What happens after your surgical procedure is over is an issue you need to discuss with your surgeon in advance. How much pain are you likely to have? Will you have to limit your activity?

Will you have to change your diet in any way? Will the surgery change your life in any other way? When can you return to work? When can you drive a car? You should have some answers to these questions even before you are admitted to the hospital for your operation, but you will need to review the answers after the procedure is completed. Some of the answers may change as a result of what happened or what was found during the surgery.

Submitting to a surgical procedure is perhaps the situation where you may feel the most vulnerable as a patient. It's hard to imagine any other circumstance where you would lose so much power over yourself. The smart patient knows, however, that understanding what's going to happen and making an informed choice about it are the most important ways to maintain your power as a patient. Surgery may not always be the answer to every medical problem that you have, but often it is the best, and, when that's the case, just get all your questions answered first.

12
Second and Other Opinions

O-pin-ion- *n.* A conclusion or judgement held with confidence but
falling short of positive knowledge.

Webster's Dictionary (1992, 681)

Dr Grimaldi was a very talented young surgeon. After a week on
the surgery service working with Dr Grimaldi every day, though,
Pete was beginning to observe something interesting. Dr Grimaldi
seemed unsure of herself outside the operating room. Gowned,
gloved, masked, and scrubbed, she was truly in charge – technically skilled and clearly in control of what she was doing. Facing
a patient and family members at the bedside, Dr Grimaldi was
quite another person. She could forcefully tell the patient what
was required and all went well unless ...

'As I already said, the mammogram results are clear, Mrs
MacDonald,' Dr Grimaldi was saying. She stuffed her hands
deeper into the pockets of her lab coat, and Pete could tell from
the bulges that she held them in tight fists.

'I understand, Dr Grimaldi,' Mrs MacDonald continued, 'but I
would like a second opinion. Could you recommend someone?'

'Dr Kowalski will be back to talk to you shortly,' she said with
a scowl.

As she made her way out into the hall, Pete was left to placate
Mrs MacDonald for a moment, before he joined Dr Grimaldi in
the hallway.

'Stupid woman,' Dr Grimaldi muttered just loud enough for
Pete to catch it.

'Couldn't we just get another surgeon to see her? She seemed to be convinced that she needs to hear it from someone else,' Pete said.

Dr Grimaldi turned on Pete in a fury. 'You saw the mammogram. It's clear. She has a tumour which is likely malignant. She needs to have it out, and she probably needs a mastectomy. There are no two opinions about it. You talk to her. End of conversation.' Dr Grimaldi turned on her heel and marched down the hall, hands even more firmly planted in her pockets.

Now Pete was really perplexed. What was he supposed to do? 'I'm only the intern,' he was thinking. He couldn't quite understand the intensity of Dr Grimaldi's response. All the patient wanted was a simple second opinion. Wasn't she entitled to that? Wasn't it likely to make her feel better? Was Dr Grimaldi afraid that another surgeon would have a different opinion?

All Pete knew now was that she had left him to deal with Mrs MacDonald's concerns. He also knew that, regardless of the correctness of Dr Grimaldi's diagnosis and treatment recommendation, this particular patient would not be happy until she heard this confirmed by another expert.

What's an 'opinion' anyway?

In the world of medical diagnosis and treatment there are times when the conclusion is positive. The doctor looks at the ultrasound picture and tells you that you are going to have a baby. Prior to that moment, however, even when all the signs point in that direction, all the doctor can really say is that, in his or her opinion, you are pregnant. As you know, in the absence of that ultrasound picture of the actual fetus, there have certainly been cases of false pregnancy.

Much of medicine is like this. And even when the diagnosis is not in question, the best way to treat the problem may still be open to discussion. Many aspects of the so-called science of medicine are not clearly black or white. A good example is coronary artery disease, where debate continues about whether surgery or more conservative medical treatment is best.

One important issue that the smart patient will keep in mind is that even the same opinion voiced by two different doctors may sound like differing opinions. The reason for this is that doctors, like everyone else, differ in their ability to communicate. You might interpret one doctor's words in one way and another doctor's in quite a different way, even when both may be telling you the same thing.

When to seek that second opinion

Now that we have concluded that much of what the doctor tells you is really an educated judgment falling somewhere short of absolute, positive knowledge, should you be running off to obtain a second opinion to back up everything that comes out of your doctor's mouth? The short answer is no. There are, however, times when you may want to consider this option.

For hundreds of years, members of the medical profession have relied on one another for support. If a doctor is unsure of him or herself, that doctor is likely to turn to a colleague for another opinion. In a large group of family doctors, for example, a young doctor with little experience in treating skin conditions might stroll over to the office of one of his more experienced colleagues for an opinion. In other words, sometimes it is actually the doctor who will decide to seek a second opinion. Often, however, it will be you, the patient, who does. As a result of this orientation toward seeking assistance when necessary, most competent, confident doctors will understand this desire. But even the most understanding doctor may be perplexed about your need to seek another opinion when he or she believes your situation to be clear-cut.

The truth is, you have a right to a second opinion. When to seek such an opinion is not necessarily straightforward, but perhaps we can provide you with some guidelines.

First, you need to examine why you are seeking this second opinion. If, for one reason or another, you simply don't trust the doctor, you probably shouldn't be treated by that doctor anyway. If your insurance company requires that you have a second opinion before it will approve a procedure for payment, then you must comply or risk having to foot the bill yourself. Sometimes, however, you have to make the decision yourself.

When *should* you look for another opinion? When the diagnosis is serious and the treatment radical, you probably ought to seek a second opinion. The difference between having your bunions cut out and having a multiple organ transplant is huge! The more serious the problem, and the more drastic the recommended treatment seems to be, the more you need a second opinion.

You might consider seeking a second opinion when you just don't feel comfortable with what's been recommended. You may be unsure of the origin of this discomfort, especially in situations where you feel you do trust the doctor but you still feel troubled.

Finally, you might consider seeking a second opinion in situations where you just can't seem to get the doctor to communicate to you in a way that you can understand. This, in fact, may be the source of some of your discomfort. As we have pointed out, all doctors have different levels of communication skills. A truly competent surgeon may not be able to explain the procedure. In this case, you may seek a second opinion simply so that you can go back to the first, technically competent doctor with a better understanding of what you are consenting to have done.

Deciding to seek a second opinion is the first step. Getting it is the second.

Seeking that second opinion

Some doctors will welcome the idea that you would like to have another opinion. In some circumstances, especially when the situation is very serious, the doctor may even suggest that you seek one. Other doctors may be insulted. Don't worry about insulting the doctor. If you want a second opinion, get one. You have a right to it.

Your first step is to tell the doctor who provided you with the first opinion. You need to be honest about your need to discuss the situation with someone else. Going behind the doctor's back will not do you any good whatsoever. Don't be surprised, though, if your doctor isn't wildly enthusiastic about it. It is true that second opinions cost the health care system money, and sometimes they take up the time of specialists who have many other patients waiting to see them. In fact, you may have a long wait to see another doctor, and you should be prepared for this. So when you make your decision to seek a second opinion, be aware of this possibility.

Your second step is to seek a recommendation about whom you might see. People usually begin with the doctor who provided the first opinion, but you want to ensure that he or she doesn't simply send you to a friend whose habit it is to simply put the stamp of approval on the first opinion.

Other sources of recommendations about doctors to give second opinions might be other health professionals such as nurses. Nurses work with doctors day in and day out, and they often have much good information about them. If you don't know a nurse, then you can call the local medical society and ask for the names of several doctors in the particular specialty. Probably the best person to discuss the opinion of a consultant with is your family doctor. Because he or she knows you better than any other doctor, your family doctor may be the best source of information about where to seek a second opinion.

Once you have seen the second doctor, and you have that second opinion in hand, you need to do something with it.

What do I do now?

The trouble with having more than one medical opinion is that, if they don't concur, your own level of medical knowledge (or lack thereof) will be of little help in deciding what to do with them. Naturally, if they do concur, your only decision is whether to carry on and be treated. You, together with your family, if appropriate, have to make that decision.

If the opinions are not the same, you do have yet another choice. You can be treated in the way the first doctor suggests, the way the second doctor suggests, or you can choose not to be treated. You might consider your answers to the following questions:

- Is there one opinion that makes you feel intuitively more comfortable?
- Was one of the opinions communicated to you more effectively?
- Do you understand the implications of both the approaches?
- Does one of the options fit better with your value system?

Obviously, you need not be alone in making this decision. You may have a valued family member or friend with whom to discuss your options. Discussing this widely with a number of family members and friends is probably not a good idea. You don't need to take a public opinion poll. Another good sounding board is a trusted family doctor. Your family doctor can add a dimension that family and friends can't – objectivity. In addition, your family doctor will be able to interpret the options from a medical point of view, looking at one against the other in light of your particular circumstances.

Ultimately, the decision is yours. When you seek a second opinion, you must be prepared to deal with the answers you receive and to make your own decision. This is no longer a situation where you might ask the doctor what he or she might do in a similar situation, because you will get more than one answer.

We would be doing you and society a disservice, however, if we failed to mention that not every medical situation requires a second opinion. In these days of shrinking health care resources we might be wise to consider the consequences if everyone sought a second opinion for every health problem they confronted. Seeking a second opinion contributes to the cost of health care and adds to the waiting lists. Some people who have yet to find their first opinion would end up waiting even longer.

You have a right to a second opinion. However, you need to be judicious about when you exercise this right. Consideration of the greater good may not be your prime motivator, but a smart patient has a high level of ethical principles and will consider all outcomes of a decision.

13

Your Medical and Physical:
Past and Present

Most of the more senior members of the hospital house staff – residents – called it 'scut' work. Pete, on the other hand, thought it was one of the most challenging aspects of his job. Taking a patient's history and physical was the first encounter Pete had ever had with a patient, and he realized then and there that it would be the cornerstone of his clinical skills.

Every first-year medical student has to learn how to do it before being allowed near a patient. No matter how many physicals Pete faced, he always thought of them much as he had his first. It was the beginning of a new adventure with a new patient. He knew the general direction of where he was going, but he would meet many twists and turns along the way. His ability to determine which were the important twists and turns were what would distinguish him from the mediocre doctor.

The surgical service was very busy, to say the least. Usually, there were enough clinical clerks – second- and third-year students – around to do most of the admission histories and physicals, but this was the week before the beginning of new classes and clerks were 'scarcer than hen's teeth,' as Pete's mother used to like saying. He smiled just thinking about what she would think if she could see him here running from one room to the other, stethoscope at the ready, to uncover the medical secrets of yet another patient.

Pete looked down at the chart in his hand. It said, 'Larsen, Charles F.' The admission sheet completed by the nurse indicated that this was an 18-year-old man who had been admitted for a circumcision. Oh-oh, Pete thought. I better be ready for embarrassment and defensiveness. Pete had already admitted one other young man for this procedure, which is more commonly done in infancy. Although a circumcision was not a rare procedure for an eighteen-year-old to undergo, it seemed to be embarrassing for those who faced it. Pete thought that it likely covered for nervousness and fear over what might happen during this normally minor operation.

The young man sitting on the side of the bed was tanned and muscular. He looked up nervously.

'Hi. Charles?' Pete asked.

'It's Chuck, but who wants to know?'

Pete stuck out his hand. 'I'm Dr Kowalski. I need to ask you a few questions and examine you before your surgery. While I'm doing so, I can answer any questions you might still have.'

Chick groaned. 'You gonna poke and prod me? I thought that was all over in the surgeon's office before I got here.'

Pete could easily have said what he had heard said so many times before, 'It's hospital policy.' He didn't think, however, that this was really a very good reason for doing anything, and he knew that if the shoe had been on the other foot, and he had been the patient, it wouldn't be acceptable.

'I know how you feel, Chuck, but it really is important to your health that I do this. When Dr Adams was examining you in his office, he was trying to figure out what your problem was. He was focused on using your answers to his questions about the history of your problem, and his own findings when he examined you, to pinpoint the problem and figure out how best to treat it. Now that you're scheduled for surgery, I need to focus on making sure you don't have any other problems that might be aggravated by the anaesthetic and the surgery itself. The anaesthetist who's going to put you to sleep will look at this history and physical exam, ask you a few questions, and make sure that you're safe during surgery.'

Pete waited a minute to let Chuck take this all in.

'That's the first good explanation of anything anyone's given me since I got here. OK, doc, let's get this over with.' He smiled. 'I do have a couple of questions. I thought they might send in one of those girl doctors. Thank God for you.'

THE MEDICAL HISTORY and physical examination are the physician's basic tools. Skill in this process is arguably the most important factor separating the truly great doctor from the mediocre ones. Indeed, although the science of medicine is a hot issue today, this doctor–patient encounter is the epitome of the art of medicine. And this art is in danger of being lost amid the arsenal of modern high tech diagnostic tools. It requires good, solid communication skills on the part of the doctor. The medical history is extremely important; the physical examination often seems less so in these days of high tech. But there really are no substitutes for good examination acumen in a doctor. Old-fashioned physical exams are useful and far less expensive than most other diagnostic procedures. For you to get the most from your health care, you need to know something about this basic examination, how it benefits your health, how it differs from one situation to another, when you need one, and how to get the most out of it for you.

The need for history and physical exams

There is much talk these days about prevention. As the cost of health care continues to rise, health care providers look to preventing illnesses from occurring in the first place; the cost–benefit of prevention, however, is still being debated. From your point of view, remaining as healthy as possible may have more to do with quality of life than with cost. Thus, any steps that you can take to ensure prevention, or at least earliest diagnosis and treatment of any problems, is likely to lead to a better life overall. The regular, or periodic, health exam is one of the steps that you might take in this direction.

Generally, routine examinations are recommended on your first visit to a new doctor, and then every five years up to the age of

59, presuming that you are healthy and have no symptoms that would indicate otherwise. After the age of 60, examinations should be more frequent, approximately every two years (Branch 1987). There seems to be little value in healthy, young adults having examinations more frequently than this, as they are unlikely to reveal much.

If you try to determine what other tests you need along with the physical examination, you will find much controversy. In general, women under 35 who are sexually active need a pap smear every year, then every two years thereafter. Mammography is subject to even more controversy. Women without any increased risk of breast cancer (family history, in particular), may wish to have a baseline mammogram between the ages of 40 and 50, and then they should have one every one to two years after age 50.

Apart from prevention and early detection of illness, why might you need a history and physical? Whenever you visit a new family doctor or a specialist, he or she will need such information. This new doctor is unlikely to rely completely on information received from a physician you have previously seen. You will also need a history and physical exam whenever you are admitted to hospital for any reason. Although your records of previous admissions at that hospital will be available, the medical staff will require current information. These examinations will be most effective for your health care if you understand what they entail and how you should cooperate.

The medical history

We will go through a typical history taking with you and indicate to you what information the doctor will routinely ask about and, when necessary, how you can enhance the results (adapted from Hochstein and Rubin 1964).

The introductory data
   The doctor will ask you specific questions about your vital
   statistics (name, address, occupation). You can help here by
   ensuring that you don't hold back. In addition, give the doctor

any records of previous medical treatment that you might
have with you.

Chief complaint

If you have gone to the doctor with a specific problem, or
been admitted to the hospital, this is when you tell the doctor
about it. This is your reason for seeking medical care. The
doctor might ask, 'What brings you here?' or 'What seems
to be the trouble?' or a variation of these questions. Answer
the question as completely as you can, not leaving out any
details.

Present illness

Here the doctor wants to know everything that may be related
to your 'chief complaint' from the onset of symptoms until
this interview. Don' forget to tell him or her about any symptoms that have since disappeared; they may be significant.
Specifically, the doctor needs to know how long symptoms
have lasted, what they're like, when they began, and whether
they have changed. A good doctor will not interrupt you
when you are describing your present illness except to prompt
for more details. Before you even go to the doctor, you might
want to make some notes to refresh your memory about the
current problem.

Review of systems

The doctor will now ask you questions about specific organ
systems in your body. The order in which this is done depends on the problem you have. These systems include skin,
head, eyes, ears, nose and sinus, oral cavity, neck, nodes,
breast, respiratory, cardiovascular (heart and circulation),
gastrointestinal (digestive), extremities, back, central nervous,
hematopoietic (blood), and endocrine (glands).

Past history

The doctor will now review the past with you, looking for
connections between what's happening now and what happened in the past. This may be very important. The doctor
will ask you about allergies, immunizations, acute infections,
surgery, and injuries.

Family history
   The doctor will ask you about the medical condition of your
   immediate family, your mother, father, siblings, and children.
   He or she will also likely ask you about your spouse. Although there is no genetic connection between the two of you,
   you and your spouse share a lifestyle, and you may even
   share infectious conditions. Tell the doctor whether each of
   these people is living or dead, cause of death, if known, and
   general health problems, if any. Your family history can reveal
   much about your risk for many conditions, as there is often a
   genetic connection.

Personal history
   Your personal history can be very important to finding out
   information about your health problems. Some illnesses are
   related to ethnic background, so the doctor will ask you about
   your culture. Your personal habits are informative. You may
   be asked how much sleep you get, what your diet is like
   (including alcohol and caffeine consumption), and what your
   habits are with regard to smoking, exercise, and recreation.
   Your educational background, occupation, and marital status
   (if not discussed earlier) may be queried. If it is relevant in
   any way, the doctor will ask about your sexual history.
      If this is a routine, first exam, the doctor will likely ask
   some basic questions. If you are presenting with a specific
   problem, the discussion could be considerably more in-depth.

   The most important thing that you, as the patient, can do to
ensure the success of the medical history is to be honest and
cooperative. If you withhold information, you are harming
not only the doctor's ability to make a diagnosis, but your own
health.

The physical examination

Sight, hearing, touch, and smell (and rarely taste) enable the physician to obtain objective information about your physical condi-

tion. The physical examination is one of the most hands-on of medical skills. A doctor will use the following techniques:

- Inspection
  The doctor will look carefully at parts of your body. Such inspection may reveal abnormalities such as swelling, atrophy (shrivelling), or discoloration.

- Palpation
  The doctor will palpate parts of your body, such as the glands in your neck, your thyroid, or your abdomen. Palpation literally means feeling with the hand. It involves applying light pressure with the fingers to a surface of your body to feel the consistency of parts beneath the surface.

- Percussion
  We've all seen a doctor place several fingers on someone's back and then strike those fingers with the tips of the fingers of the other hand. The doctor is listening to the sound this makes. This is called percussion. If a doctor percusses your abdomen, for example, he or she may be able to hear a hollow sound that would indicate gas in your bowel. Your chest (lungs) and abdomen are the most likely parts of your body that the doctor will examine using percussion.

- Auscultation
  Auscultation means listening to the sounds inside the body. With a stethoscope, it is possible to hear your heart, lungs, and the flow of your blood. When a doctor or nurse takes your blood pressure, he or she is listening to the flow of blood returning to your arteries after they have been compressed using the blood pressure cuff.

The doctor will take your vital signs, including temperature, pulse, respiratory rate, blood pressure, height, and weight.

The physical examination may give the doctor a lot of information about your health. Be as cooperative as you can be during the exam so that nothing is overlooked.

Your rights during the history and physical

You, the patient, have the right to expect several things during both the history taking and the physical examination.

First and foremost, you have the right to expect privacy and comfort. You should be allowed to undress in privacy, or with the appropriate assistance if needed, and parts of your body that are not currently being examined should be covered. You should be permitted another person present during the examination. This is particularly a concern of women during pelvic exams. In fact, many male physicians may even insist that a female nurse be present during this exam. Privacy also requires that during the exam others not walk in and out of the examining room or in and out of the curtains, if you are in a hospital.

During the history taking, you have the right to expect not to be interrupted. If your doctor takes phone calls while you are trying to explain your present condition, for example, you have the right to politely ask that you be able to continue undisturbed until you are finished.

One oddity of hospitals is that in a situation where there are several patients in the same room, people, including both health care workers, but especially patients, seem to think that the curtains are sound-proof. They are not. When those curtains are pulled around your bed, you may have some semblance of privacy, but anything you say can be heard by anyone immediately outside the curtains. It might not be possible to move out of the room for the history taking, so keep your voice down. If you have a hearing problem, tell the doctor or nurses, and they may be able to move you to another room for the interview.

When you are in hospital, you may find yourself being interviewed and examined by medical students. You do have the right to refuse to be treated by a medical student, but don't dismiss them out of hand. They need to develop these important skills, and they are not risking your health in any way. Besides, they are often especially thorough, as they know that they will be evaluated on their ability to do a history and physical.

There is little doubt that you will have a history and physical exam at some time in your life. Some of these exams will be at your request; others will be required by your condition. The smart patient will make the most of these situations by cooperating as much as possible and by understanding the process and what it means to his or her health.

PART 3
THE RESULTS

When you have a patient (perhaps you), being treated by health care workers (the people), within a health care system (the process), there will, by extension, be some type of result. Now we will help you to see some of the results of your encounters, allowing you to see some of the problems as doctors and other health care professionals might see them. Ethical dilemmas abound in today's high tech health care system. Related to that are the costs of health care and whether overuse of parts of the system may be contributing to them. Examining system overuse then begs us to ask questions about social conditions that are now being treated as medical problems. At the end, we confront death. Try as we might, it's the one thing that none of us can avoid.

14

Doctors' Dilemmas

Man is an animal with primary instincts of survival. Consequently, his ingenuity has developed first and his soul second. Thus the progress of science is far ahead of man's ethical behaviour.
                    Sir Charles Spencer Chaplin (better known as Charlie),
                                        My Autobiography (1964)

Pete had been up half the night tending to the usual surgical floor calls. A patient pulled out his IV, and the nurses had been having a devil of a time trying to get another one in. Pete's luck with it had not been any better, and after much futile poking he had finally decided to leave the IV out until the man could be assessed this morning. Then there were three calls about medications, and a post-op bleed. All in all it had been a pretty routine night on surgery, and Pete had been able to snatch the usual hour and a half of uninterrupted sleep. Sitting in the large auditorium, with grand rounds about to begin, he welcomed the semi-darkness the presenter needed for his slides. It would make sleeping for an additional hour all that much easier.

Grand rounds was a weekly ritual. Residents made presentations of interesting learning cases, and this was followed by further presentations and questioning by the assembled experts. Most teaching services had them, and attendance was mandatory for all house staff – including Pete and all the other interns, residents, and assorted medical students doing hospital work. Usually a number of nurses and other interested health professionals who could free themselves for an hour at 7 a.m. also attended.

Pete was getting quite practised at dozing lightly while still having at least a vague idea of the case under discussion. This morning the senior resident on Dr Arnold Skittish's service was front and centre. Pete didn't know the resident, who failed to identify himself by name, but he did indeed know Dr Skittish, whose antics were famous throughout the medical school. A skilled general surgeon, Dr Skittish was much better suited to interpersonal relations when the other party was under anaesthetic. Nurses and medical students alike cringed when they saw him stomping up the hall toward the chart rack in search of an unsuspecting person to assist him on his personal rounds. At least he was consistent and non-discriminatory. He treated everyone as if they were beneath contempt. With patients his demeanour was only slightly different. If he hadn't developed a reputation as one of the best technical surgeons in the area, patients would likely have kept their distance. Pete had often marvelled that, given the fact that most medical malpractice suits develop out of a communication problem, Skittish had never been sued. It could only be the result of his expert surgical competence.

The slides that flashed on the screen in the darkened theatre began to tell the story of a very sick man. At 33, Mr M was suffering from what could only be described as multiple-organ failure. His social history provided more than a few clues about the cause of his many physical problems.

A chronic alcoholic of some twenty(!) years duration, Mr M had grown up on the streets, where he continued to make his home to this day. After days spent panhandling in the most fashionable shopping districts in the city, he spent his nights under a bridge sleeping off the effects of what he had been able to purchase with his day's income from handouts. He had never held a job, nor had he had a home to call his own, since he left his mother's at thirteen. In his sleepy haze, Pete found it amazing that Mr M was still alive.

The slides continued. One after another they painted a picture of a human body suffering a steady decline. X-rays, ultrasound pictures, blood chemistry reports, culture reports, and on and on.

Finally, they brought the unfortunate young man himself into the room.

Pete woke up. Now this interesting 'case' was a person – a flesh and blood person who was obviously hurting, both physically and psychologically.

Although only 33 years old, Mr M could have easily passed for 60. His stringy hair hung limply down his back and his newly clean-shaven face had nicks and cuts as if the job had been done by someone totally unfamiliar with the proper use of a razor. His face was deeply creased, and his dark, sunken eyes had that yellowish hue of jaundice, the result of decreasing liver function. The usual outward indicators of radiant good health were all showing exactly the opposite. Mr M's skin, hair, eyes, muscles, and nails were all severely compromised.

What, Pete wondered, were they planning to do for this man who had clearly never shown any inclination toward looking after his health?

After Mr M had left the room, Dr Skittish, who had evidently been oblivious to anything but the fact that this patient provided him with a most interesting surgical specimen, stepped up to the microphone. He was almost smiling, you could say almost frothing at the mouth with anticipation.

'As you have seen, the patient's systems are in complete disarray. If they are not replaced, he will die. Of course, we aren't going to let that happen.' He stopped momentarily as if preparing the audience. 'We are planning a multiple-organ transplant that will be done as soon as a suitable donor is found. We will replace his liver and large intestine and give him a new kidney. In addition, we are bringing in the cardiovascular surgery service so that we can replace his heart.'

Dr Skittish was so excited, he was almost dancing off the podium. Pete had never seen him like this. A hand went up at the back of the room. Dr Skittish ignored it and continued.

'Of course, this has never been done here, and it will be quite a media event. But this is a wonderful opportunity to try out the new surgical techniques we have been using on the pigs in the lab.'

Pete was wide awake now. The hand at the back of the room continued to wave, and Pete noticed that it belonged to the head nurse on the surgical floor that would, no doubt, be providing the nursing care for Mr M through this ordeal.

'Dr Skittish,' she said as she stood up. 'How does Mr M feel about being a human guinea pig?'

A hush fell over the room. Carolyne Farrell, the head nurse, was not known as a shrinking violet, but this might be a bit strong in a public forum.

'Ms Farrell,' Dr Skittish began, emphasizing the 'Ms,' 'Mr M is too sick to know what he wants. He needs this surgery to survive, and we can do it. We know what's best for him, don't we?'

Carolyne was obviously not convinced. 'Just because we *can* do a thing, does that mean we *should* do it?'

'We should do whatever we can to save lives.' The tone of his voice indicated to Pete that Dr Skittish was beginning to get somewhat impatient.

'Dr Skittish,' Carolyne wasn't going to let it go, 'we have been caring for Mr M for the past two weeks on our service. The nurses find him uninterested in the whole process of improving his health. He wasn't interested in stopping his drinking, and he has told more than one nurse that he doesn't have any reason to live. Judging from his lifestyle, I'd say that he has a better understanding of that than any of us. On the other hand, you know as well as I do that we have several patients on our unit right this minute who are awaiting transplants. We have a list as long as your arm of people waiting for kidneys, hearts, livers. These people are committed to taking care of a new organ, if they're lucky enough to receive one. Is your glory in carrying out a new, innovative procedure enough justification for even one of these people to die waiting when perhaps those organs could have found better homes?' She sat down.

It was clear to Pete that she had come to grand rounds this morning for the express purpose of saying these things to Dr Skittish in a public arena.

'Are you finished, Ms Farrell?' he said, his voice fairly brimming with contempt. He smiled through it, though. 'Naturally, we have taken all this into consideration. But thank you for your concern.' His jaw twitched ominously. 'Now let us discuss the actual surgical technique we will use.'

TO THE UNINITIATED, the situation Pete found himself in this morning may seem a bit far-fetched. It may seem exaggerated to make a point. We assure you that there is little exaggeration. These kinds of thorny issues about whether something ought to be done are commonplace in a world of medicine where many things are possible. Each single advance in medicine brings with it many questions that are more moral in nature than they are medical.

- Who knows what's best for a patient? The patient or the medical staff?
- Just because a procedure is possible, does that mean it is always appropriate from an ethical point of view?
- How can you decide which patient should be treated when there isn't enough for everyone?
- Does a patient have a right to refuse treatment?

This is but a small sampling of the kinds of dilemmas that come up every day in medicine, whether in a family doctor's office or in a high tech hospital. Let's look at how your doctor handles some of them.

Medical ethics in history

I will live my life and practice my art with purity and reverence.
The Oath of Hippocrates

These words were written in the fifth century BC, allegedly by the Greek physician Hippocrates, known as the Father of Medicine. Recited by some medical school graduates even today, this oath provided some kind of guidelines for physicians' ethical behaviour for years. Hippocrates believed that a physician's moral behaviour was even more important than knowledge of, say, anatomy or physiology.

Clearly, the idea of knowing that you are 'doing the right thing' has been important to medical practitioners for centuries. In the middle of the nineteenth century, organized medical bodies in Britain, the United States, and Canada each adopted their own codes of ethics to provide their members with guidelines about what is right and what is wrong. As medical technology evolved through this century, though, such codes have become little more than vague suggestions for basic approaches to behaviour. They do not provide the answers to specific ethical dilemmas, the number of which continues to grow with each passing day.

What your doctor knows about ethics

Many people believe that physicians ought to learn about ethics in medical school. If your doctor graduated from a North American medical school before 1970, however, then he or she received virtually no formal instruction in ethics or ethical decision making. Fledgling doctors were supposed to pick up nuances of ethical concerns by osmosis from their clinical instructors. As they listened to the instructors expound on various issues, medical students were supposed to tune in their 'ethics ears' and learn right from wrong. By the mid-1980s the curricula in virtually all medical schools contained at least elective material about ethics.

There is, however, a world of difference between understanding the study of ethics – a branch of philosophy – and learning how to make ethical decisions – how to act in an ethical manner – when faced by a real live patient. Ethical decisions for doctors and patients are not simply interesting cases for philosophical discussion in a classroom. They involve the lives of flesh and blood human beings whose very futures can often depend on the direction of the decision.

In 1989 a symposium on the place of medical ethics in the medical school brought together a variety of medical school administrators and faculty. Agreement on the need to teach ethics in medical schools was widespread. (This has become a 'motherhood' issue at most medical schools.) But these highly placed medical educators had a great deal of trouble achieving consensus on what should be taught and how to teach it. Many participants indicated that a lack of both time and money, and, even more alarmingly, the negative attitudes of faculty members toward using the time and money to teach ethics, were impediments to taking ethics teaching further (Lynch 1989). The late Dr Norman Cousins wrote, 'Students tend to know more about diseases than about the people in whom the diseases exist ... these students are becoming drones rather than fully developed human beings ... they have time only to pursue the habits of grade-grabbing' (Cousins 1988, 79).

There is, however, hope. The study of medical humanities is becoming a well-established part of many medical schools whose faculty members have recognized that doctors need more than a scientifically oriented education. But even this increased emphasis on ethics in medical schools cannot change the most important part of how a doctor makes ethical decisions. What counts is not what the doctor has learned in medical school, but *who that doctor is as a person*.

Your doctor, the person

A young man or woman walking into medical school on that first day in September to begin on the path toward becoming a doctor is arriving with a set of largely formed personal values. Already ingrained is a set of characteristics that will have a dramatic effect on how that person will make decisions in the future. No matter how much education the new student doctor receives in ethics, the professor very likely is not going to change that person's value system. At most, the course in ethics, if it is well-developed and taught by a skilled teacher, can help fledgling doctors to identify ethical dilemmas, become more respectful of and sensitive to patients' values, and to look at ways of making good decisions.

Take the case of a first-year medical student brought up in a staunchly Roman Catholic home who has internalized the pro-life approach. He will not likely be swayed by a lecture given by a pro-choice faculty member. The pro-life stance will have an impact on this doctor's future decisions such as whether to refer a patient for abortion or when to let a person die. As a patient, it is important that you understand that your doctors' values may vary from yours.

The smart patient, concerned about a doctor's perspective on ethical issues, will get to know something of that doctor's background. This can help clarify why a doctor leads a patient in certain directions and can help the patient to decide on the choice of doctor. You might find out some interesting things if you knew more about your doctor's

- cultural background
- education (what did he or she study before going to medical school?)
- current and past family structure
- religious upbringing
- social background
- race
- personal characteristics

Doctors can, however, learn a decision-making process and can help you with your own decisions, regardless of their backgrounds.

How doctors make ethical decisions

No two ethical dilemmas are the same. Even two situations that may look the same are not, because the people are different.

A series of ethical principles guides your doctor's ethical decision making and therefore your doctor's recommendations to you.

First and foremost the dictum of the ethical physician is *to do good*. The reciprocal of that is *to do no harm*. This simple principle is surprisingly useful to doctors. In many situations, asking the questions: Will this do the patient any good? Is this likely to harm the patient? is a very useful first step toward doing the right thing. Dr Skittish might well ask if the surgery he proposes is likely to do the patient any good. To answer this question he will need to consider a number of medical factors. Second, he needs to ask if it will do the patient any harm, and then to put the two answers together. This will not, however, provide the complete answer.

Another important consideration is the notion of patient *autonomy*. This principle indicates to the doctor that a patient has the right to make decisions that will affect his or her health. In other words, the doctor doesn't necessarily know best. That the doctor (father figure) knows best and will decide for the patient is an out-dated attitude, known as 'paternalism.' Today's doctor upholds the patient's own right to make decisions. Along with the patient's right comes the doctor's responsibility to make sure that the patient has enough information to make a good decision.

Finally, the concept of *justice* guides the decisions that doctors make. This means that every person is considered equal and should be offered equivalent treatments based on medical necessity. As time goes on, however, and resources are scarce, applying this principle in practice is difficult. When not everyone who could benefit can be treated by a particular method, other factors must be taken into consideration. Increasingly, what is best for society is a consideration. This is where you come in.

Getting in the game

Here is possibly the most important question in medical ethics today: *Which is more important: the good of the individual patient or the good of society?*

If the individual patient in a particular situation is you or a family member, it probably will be easy for you to insist that the individual patient is more important. On the other hand, if you are watching your health insurance premiums go up, and seeing people waiting in line for basic health care, you might consider it better for society in the long run if people like chronic alcoholics who do not wish to change their behaviour do not receive expensive, experimental treatments, so that there will be more to go around for others who will make what you might perceive as more of a contribution to society. Whether this is right can only be decided by societal norms, and these change over time.

We all have a part to play in making these decisions, some of which will affect us as individuals, while others will have an impact on the greater good. As time goes on, more and more of these decisions will involve policy decisions of governments. Euthanasia, abortion, assisted suicide, fetal tissue transplants, expensive technological advances – all of these issues require collective decisions about what is right and what is wrong. The smart patient is an informed health care consumer who can play an active role in making these important decisions that will affect generations to come.

The majority of the decisions that you will face, however, will probably relate to individual problems that you or a family member might face. Often these dilemmas involve a seriously ill patient: Should the person be treated? Should treatment be stopped? This usually happens in a hospital setting, and you need to be aware that you are not alone in these decisions. Most hospitals have ethics committees to help patients and their families make these decisions. Typically, a hospital ethics committee's membership includes doctors, nurses, social workers, and clergy, as well as lay representatives and others whose technical expertise may benefit specific situations. The ethics committee can be a great help to you.

An increasing number of dilemmas that we all have to face in the health care crunch relate to the notion that there aren't enough resources to go around. Some argue that this is a result of overuse and abuse by both physicians and patients of the resources that we do have. That discussion deserves a chapter all on its own.

15

Inefficiency and Overuse: A System in Distress

'Have you guys seen this?' Jim MacDonald, senior medical resident, slapped a newspaper down on the table beside the cafeteria tray he had just placed in the empty spot beside Pete.

Pete looked up from his lunch of vegetarian lasagna, hospital-cafeteria style. Not only hadn't he seen that morning's paper, he couldn't remember the last time he had sat down to read any newspaper at all. 'Come to think of it, I really am appallingly ignorant of what goes on outside medicine,' he thought.

Evidently Pete wasn't the only one. Others looked up blankly or simply muttered 'no' or 'no time to read papers' and continued eating or chatting. House staff apparently used their free time for things other than keeping up with the outside world.

As Jim sat down, Pete could see that he was clearly angry about whatever he had read. Pete took a sip of his strong coffee and reached for the paper. A photograph of a man holding a book was displayed over a story headlined 'Doctors primary wasters in health care system crunch – author.' Pete was inclined to shrug the article off as just another round of doctor bashing, a game he and his colleagues were getting almost immune to. It often seemed to them that the media found doctors an irresistible target of blame for all the ills of the health care system.

'You guys may not care about this now, but we're all going to take the heat when we finish up here and start our own practices. I'm telling you, you should listen to what your patients are reading. Soon they're going to start believing this stuff.'

People started looking at Jim with more interest. He took a sip of coffee and started to read:

Overtreated patients, lengthy hospital stays, overuse of expensive diagnostic tests – all of these, which result in a grossly expensive health care system, are the fault of an inefficient, litigation-scared, unskilled, unknowledgeable medical profession. At least that's what author Dr Gordon Watson says.

Watson, a medical doctor by training who, according to him, gave up medicine at the urging of his wife, an eco-feminist professor of Women's Studies who is also a midwife, has spent the past five years writing his new book *Malicious Medicine*, a scathing attack on modern medical care. Watson believes that doctors are almost solely responsible for the problems in our health care system today.

'They [doctors] are so frightened of being sued that they order every imaginable test for their patients even when there is little, if any, medical indication. Mostly it's because they are so poorly trained that they can't rely on their own knowledge base,' says Watson.

Watson's book is a veritable litany of sins. He details such problems as the many patients who are treated by specialists who could easily, and more efficiently, be treated by family doctors or nurses; and how doctors keep patients in hospital beds longer than necessary simply to save them for their own patients. He provides example after example of patients who have undergone tests that they clearly, at least according to him, did not need. 'If they were better doctors,' he says, 'they would be able to use their own senses to diagnose many patients.'

Watson, who practised medicine for only one year following his medical school graduation in 1970, isn't concerned that his physician colleagues may not like the tenor of his work. 'I do what I must,' he shrugs. 'Doctors have wielded their power over us for too long.'

According to a former medical colleague of Watson's, he was asked to leave his position in general medicine in 1971 as a result of a nervous breakdown.'

Jim put the paper back on the table and lifted his coffee cup without comment.

'Can he get away with that?' Pete asked.

'He already has,' someone said from the end of the table.

'We should write a response,' Jim said. 'It's time someone told the public the other side of the story. I'm so sick of patients demanding a CT scan or an MRI for a tension headache. Most of the time they don't even know what they're asking for. All they know is that they read about it in a magazine and that we have the equipment here. If people only knew how many of these patients are getting those unnecessary tests because they're demanding them themselves.'

Jim trailed off and started eating his lunch.

'Yeah, I remember when I was doing my Family Medicine rotation, I thought I'd scream if one more person came into the office with a head cold. No matter how many times I said that there really wasn't anything I could do for them except tell them to go home and drink lots of fluids, they still demanded to be treated.' This came from a classmate of Pete's who was also getting close to the end of her internship.

Pete began to think about the discussion. It seemed like an overwhelming problem. Writers and the media seemed to be telling people that it was doctors who were at fault. Doctors had a different point of view. The truth must be somewhere in between, because the bottom line was that there certainly was a lot of inefficiency and waste in the system, as Pete had already seen so far in his short career.

HEALTH CARE IS A NON-RENEWABLE RESOURCE. Time and medical expertise once used for one patient are gone. If the 'wrong' patient gets the care first, then others will have to do without.

As a smart patient, you will not allow your doctor to overuse the system on your behalf. Neither will you allow yourself to overuse the system. Collectively, this will protect the system for future generations. Identifying a problem area, however, is not quite so easy.

The demanding patient and misinformation

Consider this. A young, pregnant woman walks into her doctor's office demanding a repeat ultrasound. The doctor looks at her chart and sees that the ultrasound the patient has already had was unequivocally normal and that the fetal growth was progressing as expected. Questioning reveals that the woman's husband had not been able to attend the first ultrasound and that the hospital failed to provide her with a picture – and she wants one for her husband. In a health care system that is funded by the government, where public tax dollars will have to pay for this medical test, as well as in a privately funded insurance system, where collective premiums pay, it seems irresponsible both for the patient to demand a medically unnecessary test and for the doctor to comply with such a demand. This does, however, happen.

Some critics have argued that the media have played a significant role in increasing this patient-induced demand. The media do play an important role in informing health care consumers, but this information can fall short of truly *educating* us. The problem is that media stories are frequently not a good source of *complete* information. Even if a doctor or researcher is careful to explain everything and provide written information, he or she has no control over what a reporter might produce in a media report. As Heussner and Salmon say in their book *Warning: The Media May Be Harmful to Your Health*, 'What is significant to the medical reporter isn't always viewed as important by physicians and scientists' (Heussner and Salmon 1988, 9). What you read in the newspaper may not be what was meant, either in fact or by implication, by the medical source that the reporter used. And this doesn't even consider the use of publicity-generating techniques by manufacturers to promote their equipment and drugs.

Other sources of misinformation that a smart patient will do well to avoid are well-meaning friends and relatives. As soon as some of these people hear that you have a particular problem or concern, they will likely relate a story about someone who had the 'same' problem and how it was resolved. It would be very unusual for two people to be in exactly the same situation. Indeed, it would also be unlikely that the person relating the story has the correct information.

Doctor-induced inefficiency

Can all the media reports be wrong? Clearly, the answer is no. Certainly, there are circumstances when the medical community can be blamed for inefficiency in the health care system. Four main issues often surface in discussions of the sources of this inefficiency.

The first possible source of waste in the system stems from a fear of litigation. It is almost impossible, however, to find accurate statistics to support this claim. A more important issue in the United States than in Canada, this fear can result in a doctor whose approach to medical care is driven more by fear of being sued than by what is truly best for the patient. A doctor like this is to be avoided.

This fear of litigation is often linked to the second possible source of waste, a lack of medical skill. A young doctor unsure of his or her own knowledge and skills can be the source of system overuse by continually sending patients to specialists for treatment that could be carried out in less expensive ways. Patients seen by specialists when they really don't need that level of care may be taking time away from those who truly do.

The third possible doctor-driven contributing factor to system overuse is the fee-for-service arrangement. Some believe that when a physician's income is based on receiving a fee for a particular service, the likelihood of overtreatment of individual patients increases. Concerned about his or her income level, a doctor might be inclined to see a hypertensive patient more often than medically necessary or to see a patient with nothing more than a head cold, when he or she could simply talk to them over the telephone – a service for which the doctor receives no remuneration from the public purse. Although we hear about this problem, there is little in the way of concrete evidence to support any estimate of its extent. There are no large-scale studies, for example, that have looked at doctors' practices and pinpointed the extent to which seeing patients unnecessarily really is a problem.

Finally, there is much talk about physician oversupply. If we have too many doctors, then there will be too much medicine, goes the discussion. There is, however, no agreement on just how many doctors are going to be needed in particular specialties.

Closing the communication gap

It would be unfair to conclude that everything that a doctor does is for his or her own self-interest. It would be just as unjust to infer that you, the patient, are only interested in yourself and to heck with everyone else.

We have made it clear that doctors are only human, and most of them care about their patients. Most didn't enter the medical profession simply because of an interest in making money, and that is likely to be less and less a concern as medicine becomes less lucrative. Pitting patients and doctors against one another in an effort to point the finger of blame for the woes of the health care system is both unproductive and dangerous.

Smart patients need to take some responsibility for closing the communication gap between doctors and patients. Look at media reports related to health and medicine with the same scepticism that you view any other stories in the media. Here are some suggestions for evaluating what you read, see, and hear:

- Examine the overall thrust of the story. If it is being promoted as a 'breakthrough' be aware that it may be sensationalized.
- Note the sources that the writer of the story has used. If there is only one source, be cautious. If the source has no affiliation with a recognized hospital or medical school, be very cautious.
- Compare the thrust of the story and the affiliation of the source. For example, if the story is about a fabulous drug and the source quoted, as reputable as the individual may be, is employed by the company that manufactures the drug, be very cautious if there is no objective corroboration of the claims.
- Consider the context of the story. If it is in a publication with a reputation for sensationalistic writing or a 'television tabloid,'

and it isn't being covered by more reputable media outlets, you can probably disregard it.

- Finally, if you have a real personal interest in finding out the truth of the story, go to the library and check it out. If you live near a medical school, the library there is your best choice. If the story that you want to check out is based on a study reported in a medical journal such as the *New England Journal of Medicine, Lancet, The Journal of the American Medical Association,* or *Canadian Medical Association Journal,* you will be able to read the study yourself. Other libraries will be able to get the papers for you on interlibrary loan. Remember, the reference librarian is your best source for pointing you in the right direction. Don't be afraid to ask.

16

Demedicalizing Social Problems

If you want to change some things in your life, you have to change some things in your life.

Original source unknown

Pete had finally begun the last rotation of his internship. One week into his family practice rotation, he was seriously considering a few years of general practice before embarking on a residency. The doctors to whose practice he had been assigned seemed to have a special connection with most of their patients. This was a dimension of medicine he hadn't seen to this extent during his hospital-based rotations. Pete was drawn to the idea of getting to know patients as people in their communities – to be a part of the community himself. He was still interested in orthopaedic surgery, though, despite the personalities he had encountered.

He was spending this final rotation in the private practice of Dr Anthony Kramer and Dr Sherrilyn Fontaine. With twenty-five years in family practice and almost the same number acting as a preceptor for medical students, Dr Kramer was an ideal teacher for Pete in these, his final days as a student. Dr Kramer's partner, Dr Fontaine, had graduated from Pete's medical school only two years earlier.

Although there were certainly days when anything could happen, family medicine seemed to Pete to be far more predictable than many of the other rotations he had experienced. Every morning at 7:30 he met either Dr Kramer or Dr Fontaine at the hospital for rounds. There were usually a couple of obstetrical patients and several others to see before beginning office hours. Just before 9:00, Pete met with Dr Kramer for fifteen minutes or so to discuss the day's plan. He had the use of a small examining room where he saw patients with uncomplicated problems himself. Dr Kramer always made an appearance and consulted on any problems where Pete needed back-up.

On Tuesday morning of Pete's second week he greeted his first patient, Mrs Walters, with a smile. She didn't return it, and instead just looked at her hands that she was wringing in her lap. As he picked her chart up from the desk Pete was momentarily surprised by its weight. He looked at the bulging contents and realized that he was about to meet a patient who had had many previous visits with her doctor.

Mrs Walters' problem today was that she wasn't sleeping well, and she wanted a tranquillizer. Pete didn't feel comfortable prescribing a medication just because the patient asked for it, so he decided to talk to her a while.

Mrs Walters was a 40-year-old mother of four. Although she now had dull blonde hair and faded blue eyes, she must have been a real beauty in her earlier years. But clearly her life had not always been easy. She sighed and began her story.

'Doctor, if your husband had been out of work for over a year and you had to clean people's houses just to put food on the table and your husband was starting to drink to numb the humiliation, and your 14-year-old daughter spent most of her time cutting classes and hanging out with street kids, you'd need a tranquillizer, too.'

Pete truly didn't know what to say. Nothing in his education or medical experience to date provided him with the solutions to her problems – and problems they certainly were, make no mistake. He felt almost powerless. As far as he could see, modern medicine simply wasn't equipped to help Mrs Walters.

They talked for a while longer, and then Dr Kramer walked in.

'Mrs Walters, always a pleasure,' he said picking up the notes Pete had written hastily.

'Have you and your husband thought any more about what that social worker discussed with you?'

'John'd rather spend the evening nursing a beer than talking to anyone,' she said looking down at her hands.

'Not sleeping well, eh?'

Mrs Walters shook her head. Dr Kramer wrote her the prescription, and she left the office, noticeably relieved.

'Dr Kramer, do you really think that all she needed was sleeping pills?'

Dr Kramer laughed. 'You're so refreshing, Pete. Of course not. But you listened to her story, didn't you?' Pete nodded. 'I bent over backwards to get her in to see that social worker. It took months. What we really need is one attached to our practice.' He shook his head. 'Anyway, Mrs Walters and her husband finally went to see the woman and never followed up on anything she suggested. The trouble is, their family lives half way across the continent; they have no friends; no real support system. I'm it.'

'Isn't that a bit daunting?'

'Sure it is. But I'm all they have right now, and it's too much trouble for them to do the things that the social worker suggested. Changing your life, even with help, is a lot harder than taking a pill to get you through the day.'

Pete thought about this for a moment. 'But her problems aren't really medical. Should we be treating her?'

Dr Kramer sighed. 'It's a good thing you interns spend time in practices like mine before they let you out on the unsuspecting world.' He waved his hand. 'Calm down. What I mean is that this is real life. I used to be one of you, remember. Medical school is a rarefied atmosphere. Out here real people have real problems, and sometimes a doctor is the only one they feel comfortable turning to. Should I ignore her completely? Would that be doing good and doing no harm?'

Pete said nothing.

'Pete, all I'm saying is that you will constantly weigh doing something for a patient versus doing nothing. Talking to her is important, but she needs more than that. The sleeping pills won't solve her problems, but maybe they'll help her long enough until finally something makes her decide to change her life. It's all I have.'

Pete had a lot to think about as he greeted his next patient, who needed a doctor's slip signed so that he could continue his stress leave from his work.

ACHES AND PAINS, colds and the flu, needles and well babies – all of these are among the kinds of things a fledgling family doctor expects to see. Today, however, that doctor must also add to the list: family breakdown, work-related stress, low self-esteem, and unemployment, to name a few. Not so many years ago, these would have been considered social problems. While social workers, psychologists and yes, even doctors, still consider them to be social problems, they have become increasingly medicalized. These are now common issues that bring a patient to a doctor.

If you are a smart patient, you will seek the best help for your problem; the doctor is not always it.

Tracing the transformation

Somewhere along the line in the latter part of the twentieth century, some of our human problems have been transformed from social ones into medical ones. Given the 'quick fix' mentality that has evolved over the years in North America, it's hardly surprising that we should look for the fastest way to provide relief. There is no doubt about it: it is much easier to get a doctor to 'fix' you than it is to embark on the difficult path toward personal renewal, which can often be a painful process. Seeing a doctor is usually not, as we shall see, the best avenue for the smart patient.

Forces that have shaped our society as we head toward the beginning of a new millennium are the same forces that have shaped our personal experiences and thus contributed to our need to seek medical help for non-medical problems.

As the number of traditional extended families – where several generations may live in the same town or even under the same roof – has declined, one of our most important support systems has eroded. There was a time when a personal problem could be discussed easily with a trusted sister or cousin. Family breakdown and the itinerant nature of the North American population have made that contact difficult and often impossible. Following a career path or even just looking for a job has made moving across the country commonplace.

As economic woes oozed across the continent, job loss placed both an economic and personal stress on many families and individuals. When this happened in the past, that extended family could often provide a safety net as well as a personal confidant.

Another confidant was often available in the person of a priest, minister, or rabbi. With religious affiliation taking a different place in family life, this is not as often an option today.

All of this means that many of us really need a friend. This is not simply a drinking buddy or someone you see at occasional cocktail parties, but a true friend.

How many real friends do you have? We don't mean someone for whom the label colleague, associate, room-mate, or neighbour would be better suited. We mean someone whom you can call upon to listen to your deepest problem, and who can rely on you to listen in the same way. This person is a true intimate of yours.

Most of us have very few real friends today, especially in our urban society where we cherish our privacy because we fear losing it. Oddly enough, however, although most of us would not describe our doctors in quite these intimate terms, we do expect them to be bound by a certain code of conduct and, at the very least, to hold our secrets in confidence. Doctors, then, make useful surrogate friends. This, however, doesn't make them ideal.

Why medicine can't cut it

In spite of the recent upheaval in medical education, with increasing emphasis on the humanities and a return to the art of medicine, doctors still, by and large, consider themselves to be schooled in medical *science*. Clearly, it is important for them to understand the biochemistry and physiology of health and disease, and these sciences are still the most tangible underpinnings of the practice of medicine. Doctors learn much more about disease processes and how to fix them than they do about dealing with complex social problems, which are simply out of their league. A tranquillizer is quite simply not the answer for your stress-filled life.

We need to add one caveat here. The smart patient will recognize that certain social and psychological problems can and do result in, or at the very least contribute to, physical problems, such as eating disorders, heart disease, decreased effectiveness of the immune system, and substance abuse, to name a few. Once the social problem has grown to such proportions that it results in a physical problem, you do need a medical doctor to help deal with the physiological problem, but you still need someone else to help you to get to the root of your own social problem.

That's why there are other professionals who deal solely with social and psychological problems. They are trained in techniques like interviewing and therapeutic approaches in a different way than medical doctors are trained. They cannot, however, provide you with a quick fix. A problem with a complex cause requires a complex answer.

Finding the best

The first step in finding the best possible help is to identify the type of problem you're facing. When you are at the point of determining the root cause of the problem, a doctor may be helpful.

If you have done what a smart patient will do, that is, developed a relationship with a family doctor whom you trust, that doctor's office may be your first stop. If you have a confidant who can see your problems objectively, enlist that person's help. If you are open-minded and decide that you are prepared to make the necessary changes and take some advice, then a doctor may be able to help you find the best help. The doctor might refer you to a social worker, psychologist, family therapist, or financial planner. These people will then be able to assist you in determining a course of action as well as in identifying the resources in the community that can help you. Many communities have compiled lists of services available.

Another invaluable source of help are the many self-help groups that have sprung up. These are collections of people who have experienced similar problems who come together to share experiences and answers. For some, the idea of a group such as this is off-putting. Still, it may be useful to explore this possibility and to judge for yourself the calibre of the individuals in a particular group and their attitudes. You may find some soul mates.

Here are some of the kinds of services you might seek with the help of a doctor or other helping professional:

- self-help groups for people with specific kinds of problems (such as allergies, arthritis, diabetes, eating disorders, epilepsy, heart disease)
- children's services (such as parent support groups, pre-school services, family support groups)
- educational assistance for people with specific problems (such as schools for children with physical or mental disabilities
- community housing services
- government assistance programs (such as family benefits, legal aid, scholarship funds for special groups, workers' compensation)
- special clinics at hospitals
- university-affiliated research centres
- home care support services

Although your family doctor probably has a listing of these services among his or her office materials, other helping professionals have more direct experience with them and can provide you with advice other than simply who to contact. Your doctor can provide back-up for you in your search for self-improvement, but modern medicine doesn't have all the answers to everything. This one's on you.

17

The 'Smart' Death

People living deeply have no fear of death.

Anais Nin (1903–77)
The Diary of Anais Nin
Vol. 1 1966

'Pete, I want you to do a house call for me this afternoon. I should go myself, but I have to deliver a baby.'

Dr Kramer was taking off his lab coat as he flagged Pete down in the hall. 'This is a very old patient of mine. I mean he walked in here my first week in practice looking for a new doctor. Now, he's quite ill. Tell him I'll be in to see him as soon as I can. He's kind of a special one, and he'll probably like you, anyway.'

As Dr Kramer sped down the hall, he called back over his shoulder. 'His chart's on my desk. His name is Norm Frail. See you later.'

Norm Frail? Pete was sure it couldn't be the same Norman Oliver Thomas Frail he had come to know so well on his ortho-paedic surgery rotation. He walked into Dr Kramer's private office and picked up the chart from the middle of his blotter. There it was – Frail, Norman Oliver Thomas. There couldn't possibly be two of them in one town.

Pete quickly rifled through to the most recent doctors' notes to see what was happening to Mr Frail. Then he checked for the time of his next appointment and headed to his car.

As Pete drove across town to the long-term care facility where Mr Frail was living, in his mind he pieced together this very special man's story. After the hip surgery, Mr Frail had gone to the facility where he now lived. Within eight weeks he was back in his own apartment, just as he had planned to be. Less than a month later the bad news started again. Mr Frail was found to have inoperable cancer, which was now in its final stages, ravaging his body. In his short medical career, Pete had never lost a patient whom he had grown to know and care about. It was hard to care about someone who dies after being rushed through the emergency room doors, unconscious, only hours earlier. It seemed like all the deaths he had seen had been like that.

He made his way to the nursing station on the special care unit where Mr Frail now spent all his time. The facility was clean and new and much brighter than Pete had expected. He realized that this was the first time he had ever been inside a 'nursing home,' as they used to be called. He introduced himself to the nurse in charge.

'Oh, that Mr Frail is a tough one, isn't he?' she said brightly. Pete thought that her manner was perhaps a bit too breezy for a unit where most of the patients were coming close to the end of their lives.

The nurse passed him some pieces of paper. 'Mr Frail wanted his doctor to read this. That would be you today.' She turned away for a moment to rifle through a pile of papers on the desk. 'Oh, here it is,' she said passing him another sheet. 'Mr Frail wants to sign one of these.'

Pete looked down at the materials she had given him. The first one was several sheets stapled together. It was titled 'Living Will.' Pete had never seen one before. The other single sheet was more familiar to Pete. It was a do-not-resuscitate form. People who are terminally ill can sign this form with their doctors to indicate that they do not wish to have CPR should they have a cardiac arrest.

Pete felt his throat tighten just slightly. So, Mr Frail had decided that he was at the end of his life, and he wanted to keep control over what happened. 'Why should I be surprised to find a man wanting to die as he has lived? Why should he want to give up control now?' Pete thought.

Unsure of what would greet him when he entered, Pete stood outside Mr Frail's door for an extra moment. He pushed the door open and went in.

'Well, I'll be damned,' came the bright voice from the chair beside the window. 'If it isn't my favourite young doc.'

Leaning heavily on a cane, Mr Frail arose from the chair with some difficulty. He extended his free hand to Pete who grasped it warmly. Then Mr Frail pulled Pete toward him and gave him a one-armed bear hug, precariously balancing on the cane for support.

Mr Frail gestured Pete to the chair facing his. Pete was sure he had seen a faint glisten of tears in Mr Frail's eyes. He knew that he himself was having some difficulty fighting them back. 'Doctors shouldn't be like this,' he admonished himself. 'Get a grip, man!'

Pete started. 'Tell me what's been happening.'

'Only if you'll tell me about what's been happening with you after,' Mr Frail grinned.

So, Mr Frail told Pete about the cancer diagnosis and the decisions he had made about this death sentence.

'It doesn't have to be a death sentence, Mr Frail. I read the notes from the consultant. I understand they gave you treatment options – options that would extend your life. Perhaps you should try ...'

Mr Frail cut him off. 'Pete, I appreciate your concern. You're young. You couldn't possibly understand how I have come to my decisions. But decisions they are, and if there's one thing I have learned in my life, that is that you make decisions and don't look back. I'm not looking back.'

They discussed Mr Frail's decision that he would not accept any more treatment from modern medicine, and then Mr Frail said, 'Pete, you're going to make a fine doctor. You have the knowledge, you care, and you sure do know how to talk to people. But I want to give you a piece of advice.'

Pete waited for him to continue.

'What I've seen over my lifetime and especially over the last few years as my health has gotten worse is that you guys in medicine are fighting a war against death. The war isn't really against disease, although winning that battle would lead to the end of the war. No, it's death that's the enemy. What's so darn right stupid about this is that you can't win. Everyone's got to die some time.' He chuckled. 'Dr Kramer and I have talked about this over the years every time someone I know has died. Anyway, what you really need to do is to think about a person's life, not a person's body. You need to think of that life as if it were a book with lots of chapters. When you come to the last chapter of a book, you get to the end. Making that last chapter longer won't alter the fact that the end will come. It won't even make the book any better. It'll only prolong what's going to happen anyway. My last chapter is already written, Pete. Making that chapter longer isn't going to improve the story that's already gone before.'

Pete wasn't at all certain that medical school had prepared him for real life and death.

A SMART PATIENT wants to maintain control over health care decisions right up until the end is in sight. The fact is, however, that the approach to death taken by the modern health care system is often profoundly dumb. You don't have a choice about the fact that you will, indeed, die some day, but you may have some choices about how and where that event occurs.

How we feel about death

Death is an inevitable part of the human experience. Knowing that simple truth and dealing with it on an emotional level are two very different things. People often find it difficult to talk about death. The word has even fallen out of many people's vocabularies, as we use euphemisms such as 'passed away'.

Until the latter part of this century, death was often a family experience in North America. It was an expected part of a person's life, and most often it took place at home with the dying person surrounded by loved ones. There were even children around, children who grew up with a completely different understanding than those who have been shielded from death all their lives.

Today, most people in North America die in hospitals. Surrounded by strangers and blinking, bleeping equipment, the dying person often has no control and is stripped of all dignity. The notion of a 'dignified death,' however, is a modern invention, the offspring of the often undignified features of the sanitized, modern death. Thus, there is a movement afoot among health care consumers to reclaim some of the control of the dying process that has been given over to modern medicine. You can't exercise your right to make decisions about your death, though, if you don't know what your options are.

Death in the twenty-first century

Surely death in the late twentieth or early twenty-first century is no different than death has been since the dawn of mankind. When you're dead, you're dead, right? Well, defining the actual moment of death is perhaps what has changed with the advances in modern medical technology.

If we look, for example, at the progress made in dealing with incidences of profound hypothermia, we can see that determining whether a person is dead is more a function of the available medical technology than it is of a bodily process. Consider the young child who falls through the ice on a cold winter day. The child is submerged for a prolonged period – much longer than the ten minutes that it usually takes for a brain deprived of oxygen to die. Is the child pulled out of the lake half an hour later dead or not? If the child is not treated aggressively with modern medical resources, including doctors who know how to treat hypothermia, then the child could already be considered dead. On the other hand, subjecting that child to all that the modern medical arsenal has to offer has a high possibility of resulting in a healthy, living child.

When cardiopulmonary resuscitation (CPR) came into widespread practice in medicine, our understanding of the moment of death had to change radically. Popular psychology would say that we have experienced a 'paradigm shift' (Kuhn 1970). Some people are still having trouble with that. Until the advent of CPR, a person whose heart had stopped and who was no longer breathing was pronounced dead. Now, medicine had a way to revive the arrested heart and to restart breathing. So, the way we had previously defined the moment of death had to change.

The new paradigm defines death as 'brain death.' Once the brain is dead, the person is dead. After a heart has stopped beating and no longer carries oxygen to the brain, there are about ten minutes before the brain actually dies. Theoretically, intervention within that ten minutes can possibly revive the person. Brain damage, however, begins to occur before that ten minutes is up.

The question arises: should we be attempting to revive everyone whose heart stops and who stops breathing?

Several considerations come into play before that question can be answered. The first is whether the person wants to be revived. This question is based on a belief in the concept of patient autonomy, the principle of self-determination that we talked about in earlier chapters. Obviously, this question will only arise in circumstances where there is a likelihood that the individual might, in fact, suffer a cardiac arrest. It is not expected that someone having his appendix out will die, therefore, the question of choice vis-à-vis CPR is unlikely to arise. But when a person suffers from a terminal illness or is coming to the natural end of his or her life, the question of choice does arise. This is the reason for the increasing use of the do-not-resuscitate order. Signing such a document has two important outcomes: first it protects you, the patient, from receiving treatment that you do not want; second, it protects the doctors and nurses from what they perceive as their legal liability in not applying available treatment.

Apart from the patient's choice, another consideration in answer to the question about whether to resuscitate someone, is based on the principle of 'doing good.' Is the CPR likely to do any good for this patient? This is largely a medical decision based on the patient's condition. In situations where the procedure is unlikely to do any good, it is a medical decision not to apply such a treatment, just as a doctor would make a decision about what drug to use to treat an infection.

It is one thing to examine how you feel about such a clear life-or-death issue, but there are other situations that are not so clear.

Rehumanizing death

Fundamental to discussions that could lead to the rehumanization of the dying process is the question of the relative importance of quality of life versus quantity of life.

In 1990 the media were full of stories about Nancy Cruzan, a 32-year-old woman who had remained in a coma since a car accident in 1983 had rendered her severely brain damaged. In 1990 her parents asked the U.S. Supreme Court for permission to end their daughter's life. Their argument was based on the belief that quantity was an inappropriate yardstick with which to measure the life of their daughter. They believed that quality was a better measurement instrument. The Supreme Court decision indicated that Nancy Cruzan should be allowed to die if there was *clear and convincing evidence that she would want to.* Nancy had left no written instructions, but a former co-worker testified at the hearing that Nancy had said that she would not want to live this way. Her parents were granted permission to disconnect her feeding tube.

This notion of control is a powerful one. Thinking about how you feel about death in general and your own death in particular long before it actually happens is key to maintaining control. The decisions that you make about this can be written down in a living will so that you might be spared what you would consider to be unnecessary indignity, suffering, and pain at the hands of any overzealous caregivers.

Living will legislation in the United States was first enacted in California in 1976, and since then similar laws have been passed in most other states. Several Canadian provinces have also enacted living will legislation.

It is your right to make decisions about your health care when you are living. At the time of your death, you also have the right to make decisions. Making those decisions in advance, discussing them with both your family and your family doctor, and reviewing these decisions from time to time can increase the possibility that you will continue to be a smart patient by experiencing a smart death.

FOR THE NEXT MONTH AND A HALF, Pete made it a habit to visit Mr Frail after office hours two days a week. Over that time he noted deterioration in Mr Frail's condition. Although Pete had feared Mr Frail's death, after continuing discussions about life and death, but more importantly about living and dying, Pete was beginning to understand more about Mr Frail's decisions, and he respected him for them.

It was Thursday at 6:15 p.m. Pete had one day left in his final rotation, and he had at last made up his mind to accept an offer Dr Kramer had made to him to join him in family medicine. Six weeks from now, after a much-needed vacation and some time with his parents, Pete would hang out his shingle. He was anxious to tell Mr Frail his news. Although confined to bed by this point, Mr Frail had lost none of his sense of humour or the twinkle in his eye. As Pete had hoped, Mr Frail was also excited about the news.

'Dr Kramer couldn't have done better, Pete. You'll be a fine addition to his office. But I hope you remember some of things we've talked about this past while.'

'I'll remember, Mr Frail.' Pete took Mr Frail's hand and finally felt comfortable exposing some of his own humanness. 'You know, I've learned a lot in the past years in medical school. I've read hundreds of books, attended what seems like thousands of lectures. I can't tell you the number of times I've fallen asleep at my desk on top of a book. But I've finally figured out who my best teachers have been.' He looked at Mr Frail. 'It's been my patients. But of course, you already knew that, didn't you.'

Mr Frail smiled. 'You'll do OK, Pete.' He turned to his bedside table and took out a piece of paper. 'I found this for you.'

Pete took the paper and read, 'It hath often been said that it is not death, but dying, which is terrible. – Henry Fielding, 1751.'

Pete looked at Mr Frail. He was still smiling.

'You know, the dying part wasn't so terrible, either,' and he closed his eyes.

References

CHAPTER 2
Cousins, N. 1985. 'How Patients Appraise Physicians.' *New England Journal of Medicine* 313, 1422–4

CHAPTER 3
Ritchie, Judith. Personal interview

CHAPTER 5
Dorland's Illustrated Medical Dictionary. 1965. Philadelphia: W.B. Saunders

CHAPTER 6
Webster's Dictionary. 1992. New York: PMC Publishing

CHAPTER 7
George, V., and A. Dundes. 1978. 'The GOMER: A Figure of American Hospital Folk Speech.' *Journal of American Folklore* 91, 568–81
Parsons, A., and P. Parsons. 1992. *Health Care Ethics*. Toronto: Wall and Emerson
Shem, S. 1978. *The House of God*. New York: Dell

CHAPTER 9
Gullens, M. 1992. 'Doctors' Behaviour Influenced by Dealings with Drug Companies.' *Medical Post*, 17 November

CHAPTER 10

Parsons, A., and P. Parsons. 1992. *Health Care Ethics*. Toronto: Wall and Emerson

CHAPTER 11

Escarce, J., W. Chen, and J.S. Schwartz. 1995. 'Falling Cholecystectomy Thresholds since the Introduction of Laparoscopic Cholecystectomy.' *Journal of the American Medical Association* 273, 1581–5

Silverman, W. 1989. 'The Myth of Informed Consent: In Daily Practice and in Clinical Trials.' *Journal of Medical Ethics* 15, 6–11

CHAPTER 13

Branch, W.T. 1987. *Office Practice of Medicine*, 2nd ed. Philadelphia: W.B. Saunders

Hochstein, E., and A. Rubin. 1964. *Physical Diagnosis: A Textbook & Workbook in Methods of Clinical Examination*. New York: McGraw-Hill

CHAPTER 14

Cousins, N. 1988. 'The Barracuda Syndrome.' *Humane Medicine* 4, 79–81

Lynch, A. 1989. 'Symposium '89: Medical Ethics Education for the Undergraduate Medical Student.' *Westminster Affairs* 2 (Winter), 1–3

CHAPTER 15

Heussner, R., and M. Salmon. 1988. *Warning: The Media May be Harmful to Your Health*. Kansas City: Andrews and McMeel

CHAPTER 17

Kuhn, Thomas. 1970. *The Structure of Scientific Revolutions*. Chicago: University of Chicago Press

Back of the Book

This is not exactly an appendix. Often, a reader won't read an appendix unless he or she is looking for something in particular. We would like you to have a look at the material that follows, as we have compiled some information that is likely to be of interest to the smart patient.

We hope that this will be a good starting point for you to become aware of the wide variety of sources of information available to the health care consumer today.

Consequently, this section includes the following:

- Associations of interest to health consumers in both the United States and Canada
- Reference books that we recommend smart patients have on their bookshelves
- Newsletters available to health care consumers
- A sampling of on-line sources of information, along with some cautions about material found 'on the Net'

Associations of interest to smart patients

We have selected a representative sampling of associations that may be able to help you to understand some aspects of health care that may be of interest to you. We have not included any organizations whose mandate relates to one specific health prob-

lem or disease as they are far too numerous to list here. There are
literally thousands of health-related associations throughout North
America. What follows might just get you started. Inclusion in
this list in no way indicates endorsement by the authors of this
book.

Canada

Acupuncture Foundation of Canada Institute
2131 Lawrence Ave. E., Suite 204
Scarborough, Ontario
M1R 5G4
Telephone (416) 752-3988
Fax (416) 752-4398

Canadian Association of Medical Radiation Technologists
294 Albert St., Suite 601
Ottawa, Ontario
K1P 6E6
Telephone (613) 234-0012
Fax (613) 234-1097

Canadian Association of Occupational Therapists
110 Eglinton Ave. W., 3rd Floor
Toronto, Ontario
M4R 1A3
Telephone (416) 487-5438
Fax [call to verify]

Canadian Association of Optometrists
1785 Alta Vista Dr., Suite 301
Ottawa, Ontario
K1G 3Y6
Telephone (613) 738-4412
Fax (613) 738-7161

Canadian Chiropractic Association
1396 Eglinton Ave. W.
Toronto, Ontario
M6C 2E4
Telephone (416) 781-5656
Fax (416) 781-7344

Canadian College of Naturopathic Medicine
60 Berl Ave.
Etobicoke, Ontario
M8Y 3C7
Telephone (416) 251-5261
Fax (416) 251-5883

Canadian Healthcare Association
17 York St.
Ottawa, Ontario
K1N 9J6
Telephone (613) 241-8005
Fax (613) 241-5055

Canadian Medical Association
1867 Alta Vista Dr.
Ottawa, Ontario
K1G 3Y6
Telephone (613) 731-9331 or 1-800-267-9703
Fax (613) 731-1755

Canadian Nurses Association
50 The Driveway
Ottawa, Ontario
K2P 1E2
Telephone (613) 237-2133
Fax (613) 237-3520

Health Action Network Society
5262 Rumble St., Suite 202
Burnaby, B.C.
V5J 2B6
Telephone (604) 435-0512
Fax (604) 435-1561

Victorian Order of Nurses
5 Blackburn Ave.
Ottawa, Ontario
K1N 8A2
Telephone (613) 233-5694
Fax (613) 230-4376

U.S.A.

American Academy of Osteopathy
3500 Depauw Blvd., Suite 1080
Indianapolis, Indiana 46268-1136
Telephone (317) 879-1881
Fax (317) 879-0563

American Academy of Physician Assistants
950 N. Washington St.
Alexandria, Virginia 22314-1552
Telephone (703) 836-2272
Fax (703) 684-1924   Fast Fax 1-800-286-2272

American Acupuncture Association
4262 Kisuna Blvd.
Flushing, New York 11355
Telephone (718) 886-4431
Fax (718) 463-0808

American Association for Acupuncture and Oriental Medicine
433 Front St.
Catasaqua, Pennsylvania 18032-2506
Telephone (610) 266-1433
Fax (610) 264-2768

American Association for Respiratory Care
11030 Ables Lane
Dallas, Texas 75229
Telephone (214) 243-2272
Fax (214) 484-2720

American Chiropractic Association
1701 Clarendon Blvd.
Arlington, Virginia 22209
Telephone (703) 276-8800
Fax (703) 243-2593

American Council on Science and Health
1995 Broadway, 2nd Floor
New York, New York 10023-5860
Telephone (212) 362-7044
Fax (212) 362-4919

American Health Foundation
320 E. 43rd St.
New York, New York 10017
Telephone (212) 953-1900
Fax (212) 687-2339

American Medical Association
515 N. State St.
Chicago, Illinois 60610
Telephone (312) 464-5000
Fax (312) 464-4184

American Nurses Association
600 Maryland Ave. S.W., Suite 100w
Washington, D.C. 20024-2571
Telephone (202) 651-7000
Fax (202) 651-7001

American Occupational Therapy Association
4720 Montgomery Lane
Bethesda, Maryland 20824-1220
Telephone (301) 652-2682
Fax (301) 652-7711

American Pharmaceutical Association
2215 Constitution Ave., N.W.
Washington, D.C. 20037
Telephone (202) 628-4410
Fax (202) 783-2351

American Physical Therapy Association
1111 N. Fairfax St.
Alexandria, Virginia 22314
Telephone (703) 684-2782

Recommended reference books for smart patients

No. 1 good buy: A good medical dictionary (both Dorland's and
Taber's are commonly used by health professionals)

When Older is Wiser: A Guide to Health Care Decisions for Older
   Adults and Their Families
   Written by Patricia Parsons and Arthur Parsons
   Published by Doubleday Canada, Toronto, 1994
   ISBN 0-385-25427-X

What Kind of Life: The Limits of Medical Progress
   Written by Daniel Callahan
   Published by Simon & Schuster, New York, 1990
   ISBN 0-671-73290-0

Choosing Wisely: How Patients and Their Families Can Make the Right Decisions About Life and Death
Written by Charles Radey
Published by Doubleday, New York, 1992
ISBN 0-385-42463-1

Health Care: Conflicting Opinions, Tough Decisions
Written by William Weiss
Published by NC Press, Toronto, 1992
ISBN 1-55021-071-8

The High Price of Health: A Patient's Guide to the Hazards of Medical Politics
Written by Geoffrey York
Published by James Lorimer, Toronto, 1987
ISBN 1-55028-020-1

Vital Choices: Life, Death and the Health Care Crisis
Written by William Molloy
Published by Viking, Toronto, 1993
ISBN 0-670-85014-4

Bedside Manners: The Troubled History of Doctors and Patients
Written by Edward Shorter
Published by Simon and Schuster, New York, 1985
ISBN 0-671-53254-5

Hippocrates Now! Is Your Doctor Ethical?
Written by Patricia Parsons and Arthur Parsons
Published by University of Toronto Press, Toronto, 1995
ISBN 0-8020-6963-0

Some health newsletters

In recent years, a number of organizations have developed newsletters designed to help health care consumers understand both the health care system as well as their own health and illness. None, however, can take the place of medical consultation.

We recommend the following as they are published by reputable organizations and carry no advertising which might lead to
editorial bias. Check with the individual organizations for current information about subscription prices.

Consumer Reports on Health
   Consumers' Union of the United States
   101 Truman Ave.
   Yonkers, New York 10703-1057

Health News
   Editorial Offices:
   University of Toronto Faculty of Medicine
   Medical Sciences Building
   Toronto, Ontario
   M5S 1A8

   Circulation Offices:
   Hillborn, The Newsletter Group
   205–109 Vanderhoof Ave.
   Toronto, Ontario
   M4G 2H7

Mayo Clinic Health Letter
   Mayo Foundation for Medical Education and Research
   200 First St. S.W.
   Rochester, Minnesota 55905

**On-line health information
for smart patients**

No guide to sources of information would be complete today
without some mention of what's available in cyberspace. We have
chosen a small sample of sites that we feel will be of interest to
you and that have enough interesting links that you should be
able to find almost anything on the Internet.

There are, however, some caveats that consumers need to keep in mind before they begin searching cyberspace for health-related information.

- Check for a reputable sponsor such as a medical school or a well-known consumer group. Literally anyone can place information of varying degrees of reliability on the Internet and World Wide Web. Just because someone has posted information doesn't necessarily mean that it is credible.
- Look for the disclaimers posted with the information.
- Look for the date of last update. If it hasn't been touched in over a year, it may not be as current as you need. Most reputable sponsors will update information more frequently.

RSNA Launchpad
   http://www.rsna.org:80/edu/internet/launchpad.html

General Internet Health Resources
   Http://www.ihr.com/

HealthSeek
   http://www.healthseek.com/

Yahoo Health & Medical Sites
   http://akebono.stanford.edu/yahoo/Health/

MedWeb
   (links to health sciences societies and associations in both the United States and Canada as well as farther afield)
   http://www.cc.emory.edu/whscl/medweb.societies.html

CMA Online (Canadian Medical Association)
   http://www.hwc.ca:8400/

Virtual Hospital (University of Iowa)
   http://vh.radiology.uiowa.edu/